Finishing
Techniques for
Hand Knitters

Finishing Techniques for Hand Knitters

Sharon Brant

COLLINS & BROWN

First published in the United Kingdom in 2006
First published in paperback in 2008 by
Collins & Brown
10 Southcombe Street
London
W14 0RA

An imprint of Anova Books Company Ltd

ISBN 978-1-84340-491-0

A CIP catalogue for this book is available from the British Library.

10 9 8 7 6 5 4 3 2 1

Reproduction by Rival Colour Ltd, UK
Printed and bound by SNP Leefung, China

This book can be ordered direct from the publisher.
Contact the marketing department, but try your bookshop first.

www.anovabooks.com

Contents

Introduction

Welcome to my finishing techniques book. I had always knitted as a hobby up until 18 years ago, when I began my career in knitting whilst bringing up my family. I attended an evening course in Design in Knitwear at a local college and then began to create my own label. Some eight years later, I took a job as a Rowan Consultant, and this opened up new avenues as I discovered that technical support was my strength. I have been lucky enough to transform a pastime and passion into a career.

I have produced this book in response to all the people who have attended my workshops over the years and have asked if all the tips and techniques could be written down for them. This book is designed to show you how to give a professional finish to your work, so that once you have completed your sweater, you will be proud to walk down the street in it, rather than folding it up and storing it in the back of your wardrobe. We have all been there, and this is why I started to teach. My tips and techniques have been developed from my experiences, and much of it has been through trial and error – I don't think my husband will ever let me forget the sweater that covered his hands and had a V-neck that was nearly down to his waist!

To get that professional look, I will show you the things you need to consider before you even cast on the first stitch, what to do while actually knitting the garment and finally the techniques you need to know to put the garment together. In the final chapter, I have offered some simple and effective embellishments that will enhance your designs and make them individual.

I hope you enjoy working through this book and that it gives you all the help you need to achieve your goal.

Sharon

The Basics

A knitter must consider all aspects of a project before casting on the first stitch. This chapter provides you with the foundations for creating a garment – from choosing the correct yarns and equipment to measuring your body correctly for a perfect fit.

1

Equipment

Relatively few, inexpensive pieces of equipment are required for either knitting or crochet. Knitting needles and crochet hooks in various sizes can be acquired gradually, as the need for them arises.

Tools for Knitting

Pairs of needles come in a wide range of sizes, and in various materials, including metal, plastic, wood and bamboo; choose a type that you can knit with comfortably. Needles also come in several lengths to accommodate different numbers of stitches.

Circular and double-pointed needles are designed mainly for knitting tubular or circular fabrics, but circular needles are often used for flat knitting where many stitches are involved, since they can hold a great many stitches comfortably, with the weight of the work balanced between the two hands. Make sure that the length of a circular needle is at least 5cm (2in) less than the circumference of the work.

For small items, such as gloves and socks, a set of four or more double-pointed needles is used.

Cable needles are short, double-pointed needles, used when moving groups of stitches, as in cabled or crossed-stitch patterns. They come in just a few sizes; use one as close as possible to the working needle size, so that it will neither stretch the stitches nor slip out of the work. Those with a kink or a U-shaped bend are easier to work with than the straight kind.

Stitch holders resemble large safety pins. They are used to hold stitches that will be worked on later. Alternatively, a spare length of yarn can be threaded through the stitches and the ends knotted together. Where only a few stitches are to be held, an ordinary safety pin will do.

A row counter is a small cylindrical device with a dial used to record the number of rows, typically between working increases or decreases. Slip it over one needle before starting to knit and turn the dial at the end of each row.

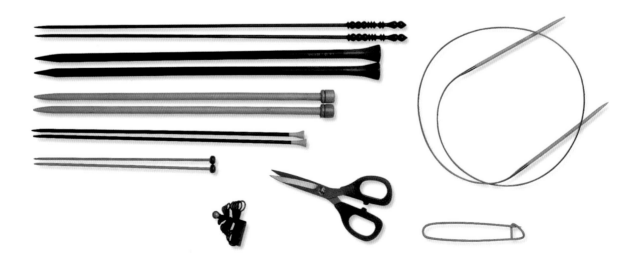

Slip markers are used for marking the beginning of a round in circular knitting and sometimes for marking points in a stitch pattern.

A needle tension is useful for checking the size of circular or double-pointed needles that are not normally marked with their size, or for converting needle sizes.

A crochet hook is ideal for picking up dropped stitches as well as for working the occasional crocheted edging for a knitted garment.

A large tapestry, or yarn, needle is used for sewing seams and has a blunt point, which will not split or snag the yarn.

A bent tapestry needle is especially designed to aid you in your mattress stitch. The bent point enables you to catch the bars of the stitches more easily.

Dressmaker's pins are used for holding pieces of knitting or crochet together for sewing, for marking off stitches on a tension swatch, and also for pinning out pieces for blocking or pressing. Choose long ones with coloured heads. Large plastic, flat-headed pins specially designed for use on knitted or crocheted fabrics can be found in some shops.

A tape measure is used for measuring stitch tension and also the dimensions of knitted or crocheted fabrics.

Small, sharp-pointed scissors are another piece of essential equipment.

Plastic bobbins are used for holding different-coloured yarns in some kinds of multicolour work.

A calculator is useful for figuring out the number of pattern multiples in a piece of knitting or the number of chains for crochet and is, of course, essential if you are creating your own design.

Graph paper is another necessary item for planning an original design.

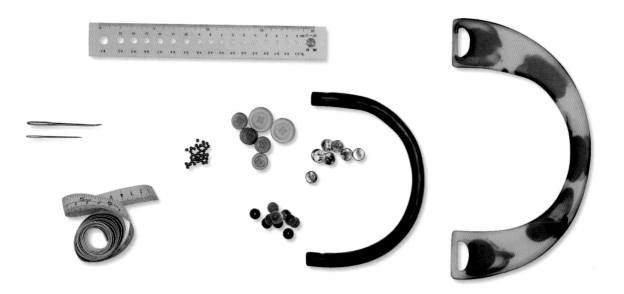

Yarns

Yarn is the general term used for strands of fibre, or plies, which are twisted (spun) together into a continuous thread. It encompasses both natural (wool, cotton, etc.) and synthetic fibres, as well as smooth and fancy finishes and varying thicknesses and textures.

Fine Yarns Very fine yarns are mainly produced for babies' garments and for lacy shawls. Included in this group are yarns called '2-ply' and '3-ply.' (Very fine Shetland shawls are knitted from so-called '1-ply' yarn, but this is a misnomer, as at least 2 plies, or threads, are twisted together to form yarn.) The standard tension over stocking stitch for 'fine' yarns is 29–32 stitches to 10cm (4in).

Lightweight Yarns Lightweight yarn works well for lacy garments. Yarns called '4-ply' and '5-ply' are included in this group. The standard tension over stocking stitch for 'lightweight' yarns is 25–28 stitches to 10cm (4in).

Medium-Weight Yarns These can be used for babies', children's and adults' garments and are suitable for most stitch patterns, from lace to heavily textured. 'Double knitting' yarns are included in this group. The standard tension over stocking stitch for 'medium-weight' yarns is 21–24 stitches to 10cm (4in).

Medium-Heavy-Weight Yarns The most popular yarn of this weight is called 'Aran'. It covers a range of yarns that have a standard tension over stocking stitch of 17–20 stitches to 10cm (4in).

Bulky and Extra-Bulky Yarns These thick yarns are generally used for loose-fitting outdoor sweaters and jackets.

Thicker Cotton Threads Various other cotton threads in slightly heavier weights are available from needlecraft shops. Some embroidery cottons, such as pearl cotton (sizes 8, 5 and 3, the thickest) can be used for some crochet projects.

Choosing Yarns and Threads

When learning either knitting or crochet, choose a yarn that feels comfortable in your hands – one that is slightly elastic so that it will move smoothly between your fingers. A medium-weight pure wool is ideal for this purpose.

Published knitting and crochet patterns will normally specify the brand to be used for a project. You can often substitute a different yarn for the one

specified, provided that you can obtain the same stitch tension, although substituting a different type of yarn – a textured yarn for a smooth one – will obviously produce a different appearance in the finished item.

When doing your own designing, the only rule is: experiment. Try a stitch pattern with different weights and types of yarn and see the range of different effects you can create. With practice, you will learn which yarns are likely to enhance certain stitch patterns, and the occasional happy surprise will add to the fun of creating a new design.

Yarns for Sewing Up

When completing your garment there are some things to consider about the yarn.

Is it very strong? Will it withstand the pulling required to do mattress stitch? Is the yarn very textured? If it is tweedy or has large knots for texture, then you may need to find a smoother yarn in a matching colour. It is hard to stitch neatly and be precise with textured yarns.

Make sure you know the content of your yarn – whether it is 100% wool or a wool and synthetic blend – as this will make a difference when you come to block and press your work.

Bulky yarns can cause problems with sewing up as they make bulky seams, so try and find a finer yarn in a matching colour for sewing. To avoid bulky shoulder seams, consider knitting your shoulder seams together instead of sewing them up (see page 58).

Lots of people have told me that they use tapestry yarn to sew seams. This sounds like a good idea because it is sewing wool and you can buy it in smaller amounts, but unfortunately tapestry yarns are not colourfast. The first time you wash the garment, you could end up with dye running into something that has taken months to knit, which would be a complete disaster.

Yarn Fibres

There are two basic types of fibres: natural and synthetic. Natural fibres such as wool, mohair, cashmere, angora and silk come from animals, while others such as cotton and linen are derived from vegetable fibres.

Synthetic fibres such as nylon and acrylic are produced from various mineral and man-made resources and can be blended with animal or vegetable fibres to create strength and durability.

Structure of Yarns

The structure of yarns has changed over the years. Advanced technology and sophisticated machinery have led to new treatments of fibres. Yarns can be slubbed, flaked, knopped, bouclé and chenille to name a few.

Before You Start

There is nothing more annoying than spending six weeks making something, only to find out that it doesn't fit you or the person you have made it for. Perhaps it is too long in the sleeve, or too tight. Whatever the problem, it can be resolved by doing a couple of things before you get started.

Knitting to Fit

Once you have found a design that you would like to make, take a little time to decide which size to knit. Don't just take for granted that you are a medium or a large – look at the measurements provided for you and see if they relate to something you already have in your wardrobe. We are all different sizes in different places, so just because a garment is a medium, don't assume that the sleeves or body length will be correct for you.

Most patterns are offered in a range of sizes. The sizes are often suited to standard body measurements, but are not actual measurements of the item. You may be surprised at how different the actual garment measurements will be:

Size	S	M	L	XL	
To suit bust	81	81½	89	91½	cm
	32	34	35	36	in

The pattern should then tell you actual measurements, either as a table or in a diagram. The actual measurements are the important ones.

Garment Fit

In order to choose the correct size to fit, you need to check the measurements of the person you are knitting for. If the item is for yourself, ask someone to help you take the vital measurements. The easiest way to do this is to check the measurements of a similar garment, whether it is hand knitted or not. First, put the garment on and decide what you are happy with. Is this garment correct in the body, but not the sleeve? Are the sleeves fine, but the body too wide or too long?

Make a note of the changes you need to make for an accurate fit, then remove the garment and take all the measurements you need.

Once you have checked the measurements, compare them with the measurements on the pattern to determine which ones match. It may work out that you need to knit the body as a medium and the sleeve as a large. If you need to make changes to the dimensions of the garment, see page 16.

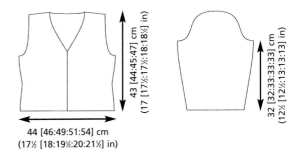

44 [46:49:51:54] cm
(17½ [18:19½:20:21½] in)

43 [44:45:47] cm
(17 [17½:17½:18:18½] in)

32 [32:33:33:33] cm
(12½ [12½:13:13:13] in)

These two pictures show actual finished measurements of a garment. Sleeve lengths are always measured from the cuff to the armhole shaping.

Measuring

1 Look in the mirror and decide where the garment fits you and what you would like to change.

2 To measure the width, lay the garment flat on the floor and measure just below the armhole, seam to seam.

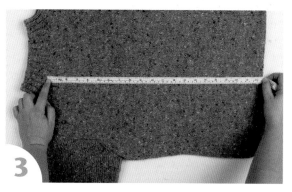

3 When measuring length, measure from the center of the back of the neck to the lower edge.

4 To obtain the sleeve length, measure from armhole to cuff in a horizontal line. Do not follow the seam.

Sleeve Measurements

To check that you will get the correct sleeve length, knit the front and back and put them together (they can just be tacked), then take the sleeve measurement from the armhole edge to the cuff. This is especially useful when making a garment with a drop shoulder.

Altering Measurements

If you find that the standard pattern sizes do not provide the exact measurements you would like, you may want to alter the pattern for a better fit. If the garment you want to adjust is fitted, you will need to adjust the increases and decreases. See Altering Sleeves (right) to learn how.

Garment Length

If the garment has a straight body, it will be easier to adjust the length. You need to alter the length between the top of the welt and the armholes. Should the garment have a heavy pattern such as colour work, it may be slightly more challenging to fit in extra rows. First, work out how many rows you need to add by looking at the tension instructions. For instance, it may say 28 rows = 10cm (4in), which means that for every inch in length, you will knit seven rows. If you want to add a half inch to the length, you would therefore need to add three and a half rows. Since you cannot knit a fraction of a row, you will need to add a whole number, one more or less than the fraction, whichever is easier. For a very patterned design, you will have to add the rows in where you can, perhaps some in the welt, some before the pattern begins, then halfway up and at the top.

Garment Width

Work out by how many inches you need to increase or decrease and look at the tension instructions. If these say 18 sts = 10cm (4in), this means that for every inch in width, you should have four and a half stitches. To increase the width by an inch, you would need to add five stitches (since you can't knit a fraction, round up or down to a whole number). If you are working with a pattern, you may need to spread your five stitches across the row. Once you have done this, keep the five extra stitches throughout the garment. For instance, when you are knitting the armholes following the pattern, it may say that you should have 85 stitches remaining, but you will have 90 stitches. These extra stitches should be divided equally and added to the shoulders – don't add them into the neck, as this will make it too large.

To decrease the width, work out the number of stitches you need to decrease by in the same way and take this number of stitches off the amount you cast on.

If the garment is fitted, you must still add or subtract stitches as described above. Continue with the shaping following the pattern, but just remember to add or take away these stitches from the number the pattern says you will have remaining after each decrease or increase.

Altering Sleeves

When adjusting a sleeve in length, either by making it shorter or longer, you will need to adjust the number of increases and decreases that create the shaping. The easiest way to do this is to actually start from scratch, as if you were designing the garment yourself.

To do this you need to know:
1. How many stitches you must cast on.
2. How many stitches you need to have at the end of all the increases, before you begin shaping the sleeve head.
3. How long your sleeve actually needs to be, from the end of the welt to the shaping of the sleeve head.
4. The correct tension, according to the pattern.

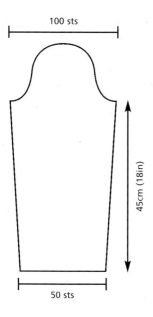

100 sts

45cm (18in)

50 sts

For example:

1. Cast on 50 sts.
2. Finish with 100 sts, before sleeve head shaping.
3. Required sleeve length 45cm (18in) from end of welt to sleeve head shaping. (Patterns will quote the sleeve length from cast on to sleeve head shaping, you will need to omit the length of the welt from this dimension).
4. Tension is 20 sts and 28 rows = 10cm (4in), which means that 5 sts and 7 rows = 2.5cm (1in).

With the information above you can see that you need to increase 50 stitches between casting on and beginning the sleeve head shaping. As you increase at both ends of the row, this means that you need 25 increases in total.

To achieve a length of 45cm (18in), you need to knit 45 x 2.8 = 126 rows.

You then divide 126 by 25 = 5.04 – this means that you need to increase every 5th row.

Tension

To obtain the correct measurements, there is one very important exercise you must do before you begin knitting the garment, and that is to make a tension square. If your tension is not correct, the garment will not equal the dimensions quoted in the pattern. All the calculations given here to get the correct measurements are pointless if you don't obtain the correct tension as you work.

I'm sure most of you have bought your yarn, and then rushed home to get the dinner cooked and the children to bed early, ready to start your new knitting project. You pick up the needles and go straight to the instructions for BACK to see how many stitches to cast on. It's not until you have finished the garment and tried it on (or given it to someone as a gift), that you find out it's too big, small, long, short…I speak from experience!!

It is vital to do a tension square, even if you have used that yarn before. How you knit is something that can change as you get older or as a reaction to the stresses and strains of life. With all the new spinning techniques and fancy yarns available, it is even more important to see how you knit with a particular yarn.

The tension of a yarn is based on an average usage. For the manufacturer and designers to produce designs for you to knit, they have to quote a tension in order for you to obtain the measurements given. It's OK not to knit as per the average, but it is important for you to know if you meet the average or not so that you can make any adjustments needed in order to achieve the correct size.

How to Make a Tension Swatch

First of all, look at the tension details in your pattern. It should read something like this:

20 sts and 28 rows to 10cm (4in) measured over stocking stitch using 4mm (US 6) needles.

Making sure you use the correct yarn and needles, cast on at least 4 more stitches than stated in the tension instructions (this will allow you to measure within the finished square so you get a true width of the stitches). Work at least four rows more than stated in the stitch quoted, in this example, stocking stitch. Once you have completed 32 rows keep the stitches on the needle and follow the measuring steps (right).

For example, let's say you are knitting a sweater that is supposed to be 50cm (20in) wide at a tension of 20 stitches to 10cm (4in), but you have only obtained 19 stitches to 10cm (4in). You may think it is OK to be off by one stitch, but those stitches will add up. There are five lots of 10cm (4in) across the sweater, which amounts to five stitches across the width. Add the front and back together and you will have a 10-stitch difference. In measurements, this means that your sweater will be 5cm (2in) larger than you want it to be, which can make quite a difference in your fit.

If you achieve 21 stitches to 10cm (4in), this means your knitting is tighter than the average and in the example above this will result in your garment being 5cm (2in) too small. This might make the difference between you wearing it or having to give it away.

How to Obtain the Correct Tension

Once you have knitted your tension square and discovered you are out by one or two stitches, what should you do next? The general rule is to alter your needle size by one size, which will give you one stitch difference. The type of needle that you use can alter your tension, therefore knit your garment with the same needles used to make your sample square.

For example: The pattern tension reads 20 sts = 10cm (4in) on a 4mm (US 6) needle, but you have 19 stitches. Re-knit your square using 3.75mm (US 5) needles.

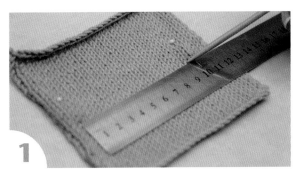

To measure tension width, place a pin between two stitches, measure exactly 10cm (4in) from that pin and place a second pin. Count the stitches between the pins, including any half stitches.

To measure tension length, place the pin two rows up from the cast on edge. Measure exactly 10cm (4in) from the pin and mark with another pin. Now count the rows between both pins.

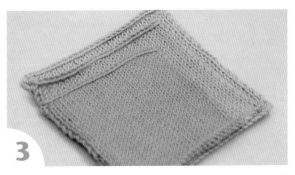

This is a perfect example of swatches that are knit too tight and too loose. The difference in tension can affect the size of your finished garment quite drastically.

If you had 21 stitches, you would switch to a pair of 4.5mm (US 7) needles. If you are out by two stitches, then you need to alter your needle size by two sizes.

Changing Yarn

If you wish to try and substitute yarns, this is where tension will be vital. Always knit a tension swatch first to see if the yarn fits to the tension of the pattern. Most manufacturers display an average tension on a ball band – if your tension differs by one stitch, you should be able to obtain the correct tension by changing one needle size. If it differs by more, you will need to change your yarn size accordingly and to check the amount of yarn you will need. Perhaps the pattern is for pure wool and you wish to make it in cotton. As cotton is a heavier yarn, you will not get as much length in a ball as in a ball of pure wool, so to work out how much cotton yarn you will need, you must do a meterage calculation.

Meterage Calculation

First of all, check the pattern for the meterage of yarn that should be used. For example, perhaps the wool has 126m (413ft) per ball and the pattern states that you need 15 balls of that yarn. Multiply 126m x 15 to give you the total meterage required for the project, which, in this case, would be 1,890m (6,200ft).

Then calculate the meterage of the yarn you wish to use. If meterage for desired yarn is 95m per ball, divide 1,890 by 95 = 19.89. Round this figure to the nearest whole number, and you will need 20 balls of the new yarn to complete the project.

Once you have your measurements, decided which size to make and achieved the corrected tension, it's time to start knitting. The time you have just invested will pay off in the end.

Creating Different Effects with Yarn

When substituting yarn, think about whether the yarn is going to change the overall appearance of the garment. In the examples above, a change of cotton yarn to a nubby tweed creates an entirely new look and feel to the garment. Experimenting with different textures can result in some interesting effects. If you are using a substitute yarn, it is always worth knitting the back and then one sleeve. This is approximately halfway through the garment so you will be able to calculate whether you are going to have enough yarn to finish the project.

Dear Diary...

Keep a knitting diary with details of all the projects you have knitted. Include any alterations that you have made, attach your tension square and a ball band. This way you will always have a record to refer back to.

Getting Started

If you're planning to knit correctly, why
not begin with the first stitch? From
choosing the best method of casting
on to selecting the right shaping, these
techniques will have the greatest impact
on your design.

Casting On

There are several things to think about that could make a difference to your finished garment, including how you cast on. I will always remember one particular lady who came to a workshop and told me that she knew over 100 different ways to cast on! Though there are certainly many ways to do it, the three most useful and popular methods are cable, thumb and invisible. It's best to decide which one to use by looking at the type of yarn and style of the garment.

Cable Method

Contrary to popular belief, the cable cast-on method has nothing to do with cables (which may offer relief to the beginner knitter). Worked with two needles, this cast on forms a firm and secure edge and prevents rib stitches and welts from stretching or distorting in shape. Unlike the thumb method cast on, this technique doesn't require a tail so you'll need to leave enough to weave or seam in ends.

1
Make a slipstitch and place it onto the needle. Place the RH needle into the slipstitch on the LH needle.

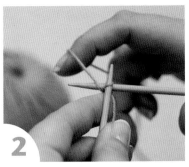

2
Place one needle point perpendicular and over the other, bring the yarn around the point of the RH needle.

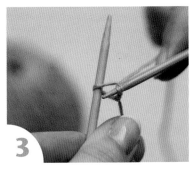

3
Bring the RH needle through the stitch on the LH needle.

4
Pull the loop through and place onto the LH needle.

5
Place the RH needle behind the stitch you have just completed. Repeat steps 2–5 as needed.

6
Once you have the required number of stitches, the edge should look something like this.

Thumb Method

This method offers a more elasticised finish and is ideal for moss-stitched edgings and for garments that are straight in shape rather than being pulled in at the welt – a straight tunic for instance. It is particularly useful when working with yarns that have less stretch, such as cotton and chenille. You use only one needle and your thumb when working this method, and be sure to allow for enough yarn at the start to cast on the number of stitches you need.

Left-Handed Knitter?

If you are left handed, it is always best to try and work the right-handed way or else you will come across patterns that are impossible to do as you are approaching from the other direction. You will also face having to alter a lot of instructions. If you have problems controlling the yarn in the right hand, try the continental method of knitting, in which it is controlled in the left hand.

Start off this method by creating a loop. To do this put the yarn clockwise around your left thumb.

Insert the RH needle into loop made around the left thumb.

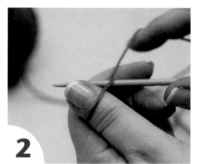

Bring the yarn around the RH needle.

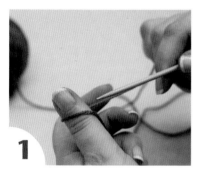

Bring the pointed needle forward through the loop.

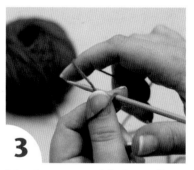

Pull using both ends of yarn. Repeat steps 1–5 until enough stitches have been obtained.

As you can see, the thumb method creates a less noticeable edge to the knitted project.

Invisible Method

This method is quite sophisticated, as it doesn't look like it has been cast on at all. It is worked with a contrast yarn for the first four rows then you change to the yarn used for the garment and work in rib, or whichever stitch is needed for the welt. It enables you to obtain an edging that has elasticity and strength. To work this cast on, you must cast on half the number of stitches that you need for the edging on your garment. You then work two rows of stocking stitch in a contrast colour, followed by four rows of stocking stitch in the colour of the welt for your garment.

1

Using the main colour, purl one stitch from the LH needle.

2

Pick up a stitch from where the two colours join with the RH needle.

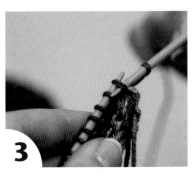

3

Place the stitch onto the LH needle.

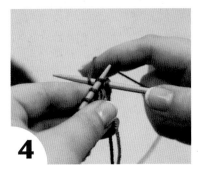

4

Knit the stitch.

5

Continue across the row and you will obtain double the amount of stitches that you've started with. Draw up the end of the contrast yarn and cut.

6

Unpick contrasts rows off the bottom of the edge.

Even Knitting

You have now cast on and you are ready to get on with the project. Many knitters have come to me in the past complaining of problems with their knitting. They say that it is uneven, that it has ridges, or that their moss stitch is all baggy, and they want to know how they can improve. Use some of the following techniques to achieve an even knit.

Eliminating Ridges

The most common reason for ridges is that your tension is looser on one row than the other; usually it is the purl row. This may be due to the way you are holding your yarn or needles, or sometimes it's because you are not correcting the tension of the yarn when you have completed a stitch. The best way to see what you are doing wrong is to try some knitting in slow motion and see what you do. It could be that you see your knitting is a bit loose, possibly on the purl row, so you make a conscious effort to make it tighter on the knit row, which only emphasises your loose purl stitches even more. Try and keep your knitting to an even tension; if this means being loose on both knit and purl rows, then try using a smaller needle.

Untidy Moss Stitch

A moss stitch can appear untidy when the project has been knitted loosely. This is a common problem and one that needs practice to be able to improve. It mostly occurs when you are going too quickly and changing yarn from back to front or visa versa. What happens is that you change your yarn before you have actually completed the stitch, so you are not giving your yarn a little pull to make the stitch nice and snug to the needle. To improve your moss stitch, work a piece and look slowly at how you do it. Try not to move the yarn to the other side of the work until you have completed the stitch that you are on, which will enable you to correct the tension on the yarn before going ahead to the next stitch.

Edge Stitches

The edge stitch is the first and last stitch of each row, otherwise known as the selvedge. Many knitters ask me how I work my edge stitches, but everybody is horrified when I say I don't do anything special, such as slip the first stitch, knit the first purl stitch, etc. Slipping the first stitch of each row will give you problems when completing your garment, if you need to pick up stitches for front bands and necks. Knitting the first and last stitch of every row will make your piece of knitting look nice on its own, but it will make your seams rough and bobbly when you stitch the garment together. Stitches picked up round the neckline will also have a tendency not to lay flat. I find it's best just to knit to the end and start with a purl on a purl row. Some people find their edge stitch is loose and feel that to knit it or slip it makes it neater. I would look at why it is loose. As mentioned in Eliminating Ridges (above left), sometimes when you see a loose stitch you automatically tighten it on the next row, which just emphasises the loose stitch.

▲ This sample of even knitting shows my edges.

Shaping

This is a technique with many different options, and it is best to use the option that suits your finished garment best. You need to consider if the shaping is part of the design and something that you wish to see. If a designer has put shaping in as a design feature, the pattern will tell you exactly where and how to do the shapings.

Working at the Outer Edge

If the pattern says something such as increase each end of the next and following fourth row, this means that you are meant to carry out these instructions on the outer edge of the work so the shapings will be hidden in the seam. This may not look so attractive when the work is on the needles, but it does mean that the increasing and decreasing is totally invisible when the garment is complete.

Increasing Knitwise

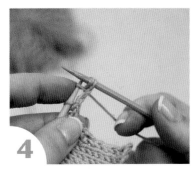

1 Knit into the front of the first stitch with the RH needle without taking the loop off the LH needle.

2 Place the point of the RH needle into the back of the same loop.

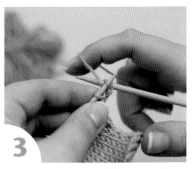

3 Bring the yarn around the point of the RH needle as for a normal knit stitch.

4 Bring it through the loop and remove the remaining loop off the LH needle. You have now made two stitches out of one.

5 You will see a small bar across the 2nd stitch from the edge. Use this bar to keep a track of how many rows you have done since the last increase.

Increasing Purlwise

1 Purl into the front of the first stitch without removing the loop off the LH needle and bring the RH needle into the back of the loop remaining on the LH needle.

2 Bring the yarn around the point of the RH needle as for a normal purl stitch.

3 Put the point of the RH needle through the loop of the stitch and push the remaining loop off the LH needle.

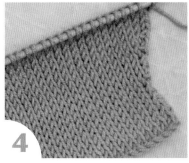

4 You have now created two stitches out of one at the far edge.

Working Increases

When you are increasing into a simple stitch such as stocking stitch or garter stitch, it's quite simple to see how many extra stitches you have made. When working increases into a heavier pattern, such as lace or cables, it is best to place a marker after the first increase and keep it in the same place on each row. Then work all extra stitches from the marker in stocking stitch until you have enough to complete a pattern repeat.

Decreasing Knitwise

Place the RH needle into the front of the first two stitches and knit these stitches together.

Decreasing Purlwise

Place the point of the RH needle through the front of the first two stitches in a purlwise direction and purl two stitches together.

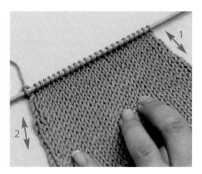

▲ Here is a sample of decreasing on the knit side (1) and the purl side (2).

Making a Stitch

This is used when you need to make a stitch in the middle of a row and it needs to be invisible. You work between two stitches to create a neat increase.

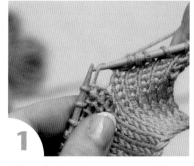

Pick up the loop between two stitches with the RH needle.

Place onto the LH needle.

Knit into the back.

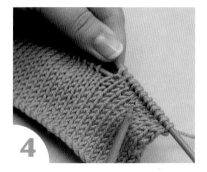

Here you can see how invisible the increase is.

Decorative Decreasing

Decorative decreasing, which is also known as fully fashioning, is used to give a little detail to a garment as shown on page 8. There are several techniques that enable you to slope the shapings either to the left or the right.

Creating a Right-Side Slope on the Knit (K2tog) and Purl (P2tog) Row

To create a slope on the knit row, place the point of the RH needle into the front of the next two stitches and knit them together.

To create a slope on the purl row, place the point of the RH needle into the front of next two stitches in a purl direction and purl two stitches together.

Repeat steps 1–2 as necessary. The shape of your project will look like this when you have created the slope on the knit and purl row.

Stitch Doctor

There's nothing more frustrating than bringing your knitting to a halt, because of an issue that you just don't have a solution for. Here are the answers to some questions that may save you time on your next project:

I have a bump where I have knitted on a knot from the yarn. How can I eliminate it? Unfortunately, you can't! However, to prevent this from happening with future projects, avoid knitting the knot in. You should always take the yarn back to the beginning of the row and cut the knot from the yarn and rejoin.

A good tip is to always pull a couple of yards of yarn from the ball at the beginning of every row to check for knots.

My cuffs are very loose and baggy. How can I improve them? This could be that your casting on is too loose, (see Cable Method, page 22). It could also be that your sleeve is too long and you keep having to pull or role the sleeves up. Always check the length of the sleeves before starting to knit them (see page 15). If this all fails then you could always knit in a strand of shearing elastic when working your welt.

The lower edge of my knitting is loose and uneven. How can I improve it? Loose lower edges are caused by the way you cast on, and normally this occurs through the cable cast on method. Instead of going between the two stitches to make the next stitch people make the mistake of going into the last stitch made. This will give you a very loose effect.

I can't find the right colour yarn in the right weight. What can I do? Have a look to see if they have the right shade in an alternate weight. See the notes on page 19 for substituting yarns and calculating meterage.

Creating a Left-Side Slope, Sl1, k1, psso

1

Slip one stitch from the LH needle to the RH needle, knit the next stitch.

2

Pass the slip stitch over the stitch just knitted, using the point of the LH needle.

3

This shows how it should look.

Creating a Left-Side Slope, K2togtbl

1

Place the RH needle into the back of the next two stitches and knit together.

2

This shows how it should look.

Decreasing

Decorative decreasing can be used at an armhole edge to shape both the neck and a shaped side seam. Plus, it adds a nice design detail to a simple garment.

Creating a Left-Side Slope on the Purl Row, P2togtbl

1

Using the nail of the left thumb, hold the front of the stitches against the LH needle and place the point of the RH needle into the back of two stitches, stretching them away from LH needle.

2

Remove the point of the RH needle and come in from the back. Purl two together in this position.

3

Finished shot of right side.

Short Row Shaping

Short row shaping is a technique that enables you to do extra rows in a certain area without casting off any stitches. It prevents 'stepping' and makes the fabric look as one, and can be used for darts, socks, back necks, and shaped lower edges of garments. It is most frequently used for shaping shoulders – many patterns tell you to cast off 10 stitches at the beginning of the next three rows and you are left with a big chunky edge, which needs to be sewn together making a bulky shoulder seam.

Wrap Stitch

The technique of short row shaping can be difficult to understand. To complete it successfully, you must start with something known as a wrap stitch. The yarn is wrapped around a slipped stitch as the work is turned.

On a Knit Row

1 To work on a wrap stitch on a knit row, work towards the stitch you wish to wrap and bring the yarn forward.

2 Slip the next stitch off the LH needle and onto the RH needle.

3 Bring the yarn to the back of the work.

On a Purl Row

1 Work to the stitch you wish to wrap, slip the stitch onto the RH needle from the LH needle.

2 Bring the yarn to the back of the work.

3 Slip the stitch back to the LH needle.

Hiding the Wrapped Stitch

Once you have made all your wrapped stitches, you need to work across all the stitches and pick up the wrapped stitches of the previous row in order to make them invisible.

On a Knit Row

Bring the point of your RH needle into the loop lying in front of the stitch on the RS.

Now with the loop on the RH needle, insert the point of the RH needle into the stitch on the LH needle.

Knit the two loops together.

On a Purl Row

  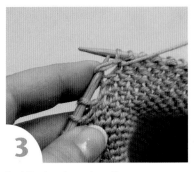

With the point of the RH needle, pick up the wrapping from the back and bring to the front.

Place the loop onto the LH needle.

Purl the two loops together.

That's a Wrap

There's no need to worry about lumpy or holey work with this technique. Hiding the wrap stitches makes the shaping invisible and will give you the professional finish you will be proud of.

Shoulder Shaping Exercise

It's not uncommon for some people to have difficulty understanding how to put the information into practice when following shoulder shapings in a pattern. Here are some typical pattern instructions for left front shoulder shaping, and then an amended version to show how to use short row shaping.

Typical Pattern Instructions

For example, the pattern could read:

1. Cast off 8 sts at beg of next and foll alt row.

2. Work 1 row.

3. Cast off rem 8 sts.

Instructions for Making Shoulder

Bind on 24 sts and work 10 rows in St st.

Next row: Knit across all sts (this is where you would be casting off your first 8 sts).

Foll row: P16, wrap st (slip next st purlwise, place yarn to the back, slip st back onto left hand needle, turn work making sure yarn stays to the back).

Foll row: K16.

Foll row: P8, wrap st (slip next st purlwise, place yarn to the back, slip st back onto left hand needle, turn work making sure yarn stays to the back).

Foll row: K8.

Purl across all stitches and when you come to a wrapped stitch, pick up the loop on the right side of the work and place on left hand needle and purl together with next stitch.

Leave stitches on a needle and graft together with other shoulder (see page 44).

Shoulder Seams

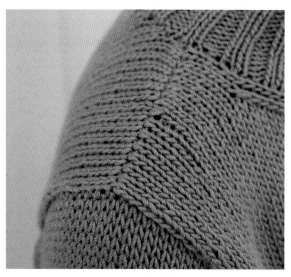

▲ Here you can see a smooth shoulder seam that has been knitted together.

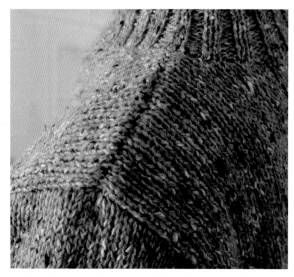

▲ Here is a more bulky seam, which when made with an even thicker yarn can become quite unsightly.

Joining in Yarn

Have you ever knit halfway through a row only to discover that you've run out of yarn? Never join yarn in the middle of the row as it will always show when the garment is complete. To calculate if you have enough yarn to do an entire row, simply see if you have enough to equal three times the width of the knitting.

Joining a New Ball

1

Simply loop the new yarn around the needle and knit in the normal way using only the new yarn.

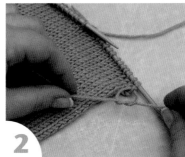

2

Once you have done a few stitches with the new yarn, go back to the edge and simply tie the old and new yarns together in a knot.

Yarn Lengths

As mentioned, it is always a good idea to have a length of yarn three times the width of your row free from the ball, so you can check before starting a new row for joins in the yarn. If you see a knot in this length, it will allow you to cut and rejoin the yarn before you start the row and prevent you from finding a pesty knot when you are in the middle of a row.

Joining in New Colours on Striped Work

A good tip when working with stripes is to work on a circular needle, but be sure to work backwards and forwards and NOT on the round. Then, if you find the colour you need next is at the other end of the row, simply push the stitches to the other end of the needle and work the other way. You may find yourself doing another knitting row because of this, but as long as you are working in stocking stitch this will be fine.

If you still have to join in a new colour for the next stripe, weave the new colour in several stitches before the end of the row you are about to finish to eliminate all ends. This should be done approximately 10 stitches before the end of the row you are about to complete, when you need to change colour on the following row.

Joining a New Colour on Striped Work

1

Lay the new colour across the yarn that you are working with.

2

Knit normally with the existing yarn for one stitch.

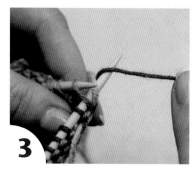

3

Carry the new yarn along on every alternate stitch by laying it across the tip of the RH needle, then bring the existing yarn around the tip of that needle as well.

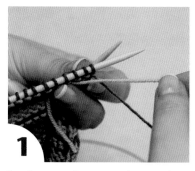

4

Bring the point of the RH needle through the stitch as though working a normal knit stitch, leaving the new yarn at the back of work. Work this step every alternative stitch to the end of the row.

5

Work with the new yarn on the next row. Trim any loose ends.

▲ Above is a sample of coloured work on a circular needle.

Eliminating Excess Ends

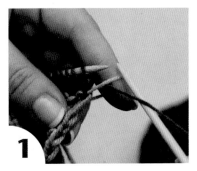

1

2

Another way of eliminating excess ends is to carry the yarn you are not using up the side of your work. Place it over the yarn you're about to work with, then continue to work with the new yarn in normal fashion.

Follow this step every two rows. You can see how the yarn has been carried up the side, which will help eliminate any ends.

Casting Off

Once you have completed knitting a piece, the final step is to cast off. It is best to cast off with the right side facing you and in the stitch and colour you have finished with. If you are working several colours in the row, it is still best to change the colours as you cast off. When working in rib, for a neckband for instance, you should cast off in rib. This allows the edge to have more elasticity along its length to match the rib. Have you ever worked a neckband, cast off and then struggled to fit the garment over your head? This is a common mistake that often occurs when you do not cast off in rib or if you cast off too tightly. Sometimes, even if you do all the right things, the neckband is still too small, in which case try using a larger needle to cast off.

Casting Off Without the Point

1 Cast off until the last stitch is on the LH needle. Place the point of the RH needle into the row, below the last stitch on your LH needle.

2 Knit.

3 Pull the strand of yarn away from the knitted piece to tighten the loop. Fasten off the last stitch.

4 Here you can see the cast-off edge without any unsightly points.

Garment Assembly

If you rush the sewing and bulk the seams when you put the garment together, it may dissuade you from knitting again. The techniques in this chapter, from seaming to sewing in colourwork, give a garment the professional touch it deserves.

3

Finishing

You have bound off that last stitch and you congratulate yourself on a job well done. Two seconds later, you decide to put it together to wear it in the morning, or give it to the person who is waiting for it. You sit there quickly sewing up the seams – and there you have it, one finished garment! Or maybe you do all that knitting, but then leave it in a bag at the back of a cupboard completely forgotten until you stumble upon it months later while doing some spring cleaning. Why do we do all that work and then not finish the item properly, or at all? We knitters do have some funny ways!

Well, I'm here to help you with that finishing process and hopefully inspire you to give it the time it deserves. After all, it is the time and care that you put in now that makes all your hours of knitting look something special.

Sewing in the Ends

You are now faced with four or five knitted pieces that don't look too inspiring in their present state. There may be lots of ends where you have joined new balls of yarn or changed colour and these will need sewing in. This job is certainly not a quick one, but it is important.

Finishing Ends of Yarn Joins

What should you do when you are left with the ends to sew in after joining in a new ball of yarn? Leave these until you have completed the seams and then feed them into the seam. Remember, the more you can get into the seams, the better. If you have a heavily striped garment, see the notes on page 36 for eliminating the amount of ends you have. It's best to divide the ends between being sewn into the work and being sewn into the seam.

▲ Sew all ends of yarn into the seams to complete.

Means to an End

What to do when you're faced with dozens and dozens of ends? Try completing each piece as you finish it; this will make it less daunting. Always use a fresh piece of yarn for your seams, then sew in the ends you have from joining a new ball of yarn afterwards, into the seam.

Intarsia

If your knitting is colourwork, you could be faced with lots of ends to sew in. The ends are best sewn in one by one (I have known it to take up to two weeks of evenings to complete).

When you have knitted an intarsia garment, you could potentially face something like this. It's important to keep the colours together and keep the contrast colours in their own area – never take them into the background.

Working one end at a time, weave the needle into the back of four to five stitches, making sure you split the yarn rather than going under it. This will give you extra friction and help stop the ends from popping out.

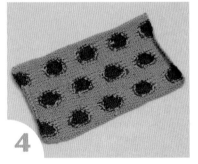

Go back up the other way about half the distance, pull the fabric slightly to secure the yarn and trim the ends.

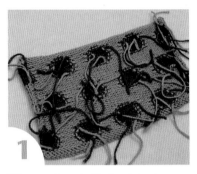

At the end of this technique, your finished project should look something like this.

Colour Fast

Don't get tangled up or confused by extra yarn balls and odd ends getting in the way of your work. When working intarsia, keep your knitting organised by placing all the balls, bobbins or skeins in a container or basket next to you. Having everything you will need in one place can save you a lot of time and will keep things simple. It's also helpful to keep yarn ends out of the way by pinning them back. The more contrasting your choice of yarns, the easier they'll be to manage.

Blocking

Now you have sewn in all the ends, you are ready to block your work. What is blocking? It is the careful pinning out of all the pieces onto a flat surface to enable you to check the shape and measurements of your finished garment. Each piece is then steamed or pressed to flatten all the edges. Blocking enables you to get all the edges nice and flat, as there is nothing worse than trying to sew a seam while struggling with an edge that keeps curling. If you do a lot of knitting and have learnt how blocking benefits the finished appearance of your garment, you may want to make a blocking board. You will need a piece of hardboard, some medium weight wadding and a piece of checked fabric to cover.

Using a Blocking Board

Once you have your blocking board (see below), lay your garment out to fit the measurements required. If your knitting has come out slightly smaller, you may be able to gain some width (if you have made a tension swatch, you won't have this problem). Lay out the garments, right side facing down, using the checkered fabric on your blocking board as a guide for pinning the garment straight. This is particularly useful when working with a piece that is twisted or curled. Steam or press the piece.

Laying Out the Garment

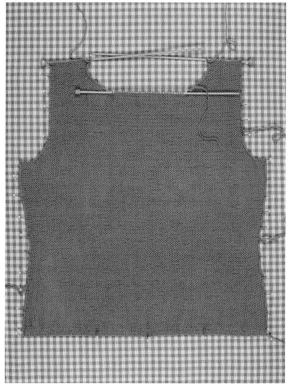

▲ Here you see a piece pinned out on a blocking board.

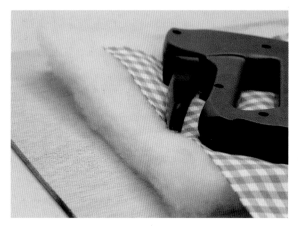

▲ To make your blocking board simply cover the board with the wadding then the checked fabric and staple gun it to the back. Make sure your checked fabric is straight and pulled nice and tight so it is smooth and firm.

Pockets

Although this process may seem trivial, the best placement of pockets seems to flatter the figure and accent all the right curves, while misplaced pockets can be very unforgiving.

Placing Pockets

When placing a pocket lining or patch pocket on the front of a garment it is really important to get it straight. To do this you need to run a guide thread using contrast yarn and then use slip stitch to sew the pocket into place.

For knitted in pockets, run a contrast colour evenly along the stitches on the wrong side of the work and slip stitch the pocket along that line, working on the wrong side.

With a patch pocket, place a running stitch in a contrast yarn to show the position of the pocket on the right side of the work. Working on the right side, mattress stitch (see page 54) the pocket into place.

Pocket Play

Make sure all pieces are blocked before positioning your pockets. For easy placing of patch pockets, place the lower edge of the pocket at the top of the welt. This will ensure that you have a clean, straight edge.

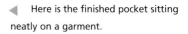 Here is the finished pocket sitting neatly on a garment.

Grafting

Grafting is a technique for joining two pieces of knitting together that have not been cast off, forming an invisible seam. There are two main techniques: sewing together or knitting together. The most effective place for grafting is on the shoulder seam as it enables the garment to lay flat. The sewing technique leads to a slightly flatter result, but I find the knitting technique is the easiest to master.

Grafting by Knitting Technique

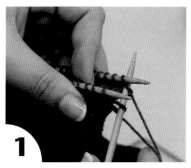

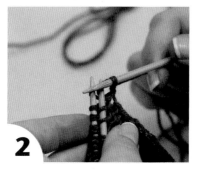

1 Putting the right sides together, put the point of the RH needle into the front of the first stitch from each needle.

2 Knit both stitches together using both yarns for the first stitch only.

Knit another two stitches together as shown in step 1, this time just using one of the yarns.

3 Cast off the first stitch over the second stitch as normal.

Continue working steps 1–3 across all the stitches.

Grafting by Sewing

1 Lay the pieces onto a flat surface and thread a sewing needle. Bring your embroidery needle from front to back into the first stitch and up into the next stitch on the knitting needle.

2 Now bring the needle into the stitch on the top half from front to back of the knitting and up into the next stitch on the knitting needle.

3 Pull the stitches evenly to get the same tension as the rest of the fabric.

Picking Up Stitches

Picking up stitches can be one of the most daunting things to knitters. You need to be able to pick up stitches in order to complete a neckband, collar, pocket tops, front bands, armhole bands and more, so it is a crucial technique to master.

Picking Up Stitches Around the Neck

Have you ever followed instructions to pick up and knit 46 stitches along the left side of neck, but finished with 46 stitches on your needles and 4cm (1⅜in) still to go? You may have tried to eliminate any holes but in the end have too many stitches. It's not a bad thing to have extra stitches, but keep a note of how many there are and adjust on your first row of rib.

1. Mark out the area around the neck into even spaces.

2. Place the needle in the space between the edge stitch and the next stitch.

3. Using yarn, place the yarn around the needle and knit.

4. Work along each stitch, missing one every three stitches.

5. If you have a hole lying below or it's very loose when you pick up a stitch, slip the stitch onto a spare needle and knit into the back of it. This will help close the gap.

6. When you get to the spot where you are about to knit the stitches on the holder at the front of the neck, it is quite a jump from where you are to where the stitches on the holder are. It's best to pick up one of the vertical stitches to ease around the curve.

Front Bands

There are three main techniques for the front bands of a cardigan, and different designers have different preferences. I prefer picking up the stitches for a front band, as this gives a tidier edge.

Picking Up for a Front Band

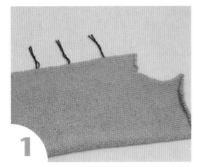

Divide the front edge into even spaces.

Pick up the stitches in the same way as shown for the neckband on page 45.

In order to keep the correct tension, pick up three consecutive stitches and then miss one.

Sewn On Bands

Band Aid

Always make sure that both bands have exactly the same number of rows. This will ensure that you will finish with a beautifully fitting garment that sits nicely and doesn't look out of shape.

When knitting your front band vertically, it is best to increase by an extra stitch on the edge of the garment and on the edge of the band.

Sew together by using flat seam or mattress stitch (see page 54). When stitching the band into place, put a slight tension onto it so it is stretched into place.

Knitting in the Front Bands

Though it is possible to knit your front bands as you knit your fronts, you don't get a tight tension, which may cause the bands to be loose or relaxed. However, it does have its advantages in that you don't have to fiddle around with picking up stitches or sewing on bands.

Joining Two Bands Together

If the pattern asks you to make two front bands, you are then faced with the dilemma of how to join them together. Try grafting them together; the technique shown here is for bands knitted in rib.

Grafting Bands

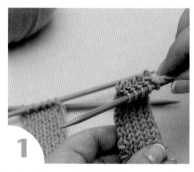

Using 3.75mm (US 5) double-pointed needles, put all the knit stitches of one band onto one needle.

Put the purl stitches onto another double-pointed needle on each band.

With right sides together and using the grafting by knitting technique (see page 44), graft the inside stitches together.

Repeat step 3 with the outer stitches.

Cast off as you go.

The finished joined band.

Buttonholes

Choosing a method for your buttonholes will depend on how big your button is. The two row buttonhole technique is the most versatile, as you can cast off as many or as few stitches as you need to make the relevant size. The eyelet technique is very quick and neat, but will only go up to the size the yarn and needle will allow. Look out for the special technique that will eliminate the unsightly bar you normally get in the two row buttonhole – from now on your buttonholes will be revolutionised!

Two Row Buttonhole

  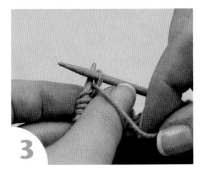

On the first row, cast off the amount of required stitches to make the size of buttonhole needed. Complete the row and work back on the next row to the cast off stitches.

Turn the work and cast on one stitch by inserting the point of the RH needle into the first stitch on the LH needle. Now using the cable method (placing the RH needle behind the previous cast on stitch, see page 22), cast on the same number of stitches that you cast off on the previous row.

Before placing the last cast on stitch onto the left needle, bring the yarn between the two needles to the front of the work to stop a loop from forming. Turn the work back to the original side and work until the end of the row. On the following row, when working across the top of the buttonhole, work into the back of the first cast on stitch.

Small Eyelet Buttonhole

Work to the required position of the buttonhole and bring the yarn forward.

Work two stitches together.

Work to the end of the row; this is how it should look.

Large Eyelet Buttonhole

▲ To make the eyelet larger, bring the yarn around the needle twice and work two stitches together as for the small eyelet. Work two stitches together.

Choosing Buttons

You can choose buttons to make a striking contrast to your garment or you may choose a button to be more subtle. Think about the size of the button with the weight of the yarn in mind. If the button is too heavy, it will make the bands hang down and lose shape. Always take a sample of the yarn with you when choosing your buttons.

Placing and Sewing On Buttons

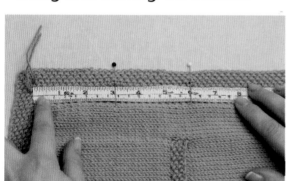

▲ Measure the position of the first two buttons 1cm (⅜in) from the lower edge and 1cm (⅜in) from the neck edge and mark with a thread. Using a tape measure work out the spacing evenly for the number of buttons. In this example, they will be placed every 8cm (3⅜in). If the band is knitted vertically, as this one is, you can count the number of rows to get the correct spacings and match the buttonhole band.

Placing your buttons is also a vital part of the overall appearance of your garment. The spacing is important yet so many designs just say you should place one button 1cm (⅜in) from the top and one button 1cm (⅜in) from the lower edge, with six evenly spaced between. The first step is to complete your button band, then mark each button position with a thread, spacing them evenly. If you have chosen to pick up and knit your band it is better to calculate the number of stitches between the buttonholes to get the positioning even.

For example:
1. You have picked up 100 stitches for your band.
2. You need eight buttonholes in total.
3. The first buttonhole is 3 stitches from the top, the second buttonhole is 3 stitches from the bottom, and each buttonhole runs over 2 stitches.
4. This leaves 90 stitches and 6 buttonholes.
5. The buttons themselves will take up 12 stitches so 90 − 12 = 78 left.
6. You have seven spaces, so divide 78 by 7 = 11 with one remaining.

Facings and Hems

It's quite nice not to have any welts showing at times, but a garment needs something to weigh it down and a place to put the buttonholes. Facings and hems can be the answer: you can choose a contrasting yarn to make a feature of them, as we have done in this example. They are also useful when you wish to line the garment, and especially useful in long jackets and coats.

Basic Hems

1 Pick up stitches on the right side of the work as shown on page 45. Knit one row, and this will be the hem row.

2 Now make a stocking stitch hem: I recommend one approximately 2.5cm (1in) deep.

3 Stitch down the hem using slip stitch.

Mitre Corners

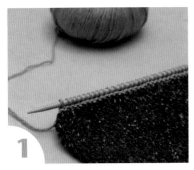

1 When making a jacket you need to mitre the corners where the front bands meet the hemlines. To mitre a corner simply decrease the first stitch on every row at the edge where it will meet another hemline.

2 Mattress stitch (see page 54) the two edges together.

Placing Buttonholes in Facings

Frequently-used buttonholes can endure damage and will often lose their shape. Using facings will provide a neat and sturdy edge. When placing buttonholes on a garment with a facing, be sure to make matching buttonholes on both sides of the hemline. This handy technique will reinforce the strength of the buttonholes ensuring that they are kept neat and even.

Creating Buttonholes

▲ Place the buttonholes, calculating their position as described on page 49. When working the hem, knit until you've reached a point that is level with the buttonhole on the body and make a hole to match.

You may wish to stitch around the buttonhole so that both fabrics are joined together.

Match Point

If you're unsure about the size of your buttonhole, make sure that it matches the size of your button. It's always best to have the buttonhole slightly smaller as they will generally stretch with use.

Zips

When using a zip to fasten a garment, it's always worth buying one at the same time as you purchase your yarn. This will allow you to match the colour and acquire the length you need. It can save you time too, as trying to find a zip to match after your garment is completed can be difficult.

Placing a Zip

1

Open the zip and pin it into place, bringing the edge of the garment as close to the teeth as possible.

2

Using small stitches, backstitch the zip into place, with the right side of the work facing.

3

Slip stitch the edge of the zip into place on the wrong side of the work.

Facing for a Zip

I recommend covering up the wrong side of the zip, as they are normally on jackets that will flap open and show all the stitching. Work in the yarn the garment has been made in and make a strip of knitting approximately 2.5cm (1in) wide. You could make it in either stocking or moss stitch. Slip stitch into place for a smart end result.

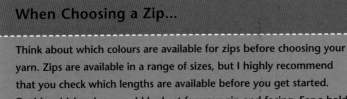

When Choosing a Zip...

Think about which colours are available for zips before choosing your yarn. Zips are available in a range of sizes, but I highly recommend that you check which lengths are available before you get started. Decide which colour would be best for your zip and facing. For a bold look, contrasting colours make the strongest statement.

Seams

It is really important when considering seams to choose the best sewing technique to suit the type of edge you are piecing together. Do not simply decide that you always use mattress stitch or back stitch – there are many other equally effective and attractive alternatives to consider.

Mattress Stitch

Mattress stitch, which is also sometimes called ladder stitch, is an invisible seam that joins two stitches together, one from each side, to make one. This stitch is, by far, the best when it comes to piecing colourwork together, particularly as it is worked row by row and also on the right side. It works like magic when piecing stripes together! The other advantage to this technique is that you can use any colour thread and it won't show.

Basic Mattress Stitch

1

Bring the needle from back to front between the edge stitch and the first stitch on both pieces of work. Be careful not to knot your yarn.

2

Take your needle back into the same stitch the yarn has come from and move up one row, giving you one little bar on your needle.

3

Continue to stitch in and out, working the corresponding stitch on the other piece row by row.

4

On one colourwork, you can go two rows at a time, rather than just one.

5

Every 5cm (2in) pull both ends of the thread to close the seam.

6

The seam becomes invisible and you will be unable to see contrasting yarns. Once the seam is complete, go back and secure the other end of the yarn into place.

Mattress on Rib

1

Work in the same technique as for the knit side on the previous page, but catch the bars of the purl stitches.

Mattress on Purl

1

On k2, p2 rib, bring the needle up between the two knit stitches on each side and work mattress stitch, as described on page 54.

2

The rib will continue round without showing a seam.

Joining Bound Off Edge to Bound Off Edge

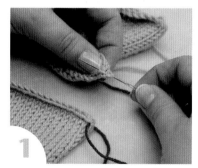

1

Bring the sewing needle up from the back to the front of the work and into the first stitch of each piece to be joined.

2

Take the needle back into the same stitch that the yarn has come from and under the next stitch of the first piece.

3

Work as for the previous step on the other piece of work.

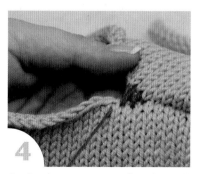

4

Continue steps 1–2 across all stitches. Pull the yarn gently to complete the seam.

Stitch Tip

Mattress stitch can be worked either a half stitch or a whole stitch from the edge. Always use a blunt needle for sewing up to avoid splitting the yarn. Lay the pieces to be joined next to one another carefully on a table or on a flat surface before you begin. And don't forget that this stitch will become invisible once it has been pulled tight, hiding the join and all traces of yarn.

Grafting Vertical to Horizontal

This technique could be used when joining a drop shoulder sleeve to the side of the body. It is a mix of the techniques shown for mattress stitch (see page 54), but when working with vertical stitches (which could be the side of a body) and horizontal stitches (which could be cast off stitches for the top of a sleeve), you must be careful of the spacing. A stitch is wider than it is long, so you wouldn't want to take every horizontal stitch to every row.

Work by going under one whole horizontal stitch and one vertical row.

Space the stitching out by doing three rows to every two stitches.

Pull the thread gently every 5cm (2in) to complete the seam.

Sewing In Sleeves

Sewing in sleeves is another tricky area. The best technique to use all depends on which type of sleeve head you have to work with. The most important thing to get right when sewing in a drop sleeve is to get it positioned correctly. You can either sew it in with mattress stitch or knit off the sleeve with the side edge of your sweater, which gives an extremely neat finish.

Sewing a Drop Sleeve

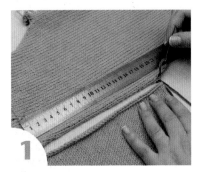

Safety pin the centre of the sleeve to the shoulder seam, place a marker to show the width of the sleeve on the body and measure.

Measure down from the shoulder seam to match the same depth for the sleeve.

Using mattress stitch as shown in Grafting Vertical to Horizontal (above), stitch into place.

Flat Seam

A flat seam is achieved with overstitch. This is best used when joining a buttonband, collar or some welts, especially with moss-stitched edgings. This seam is perfect for moss stitch because you slip the bobbles over the edge.

Working from back to front, come through the bobbled edge of the moss stitch and pull tight. Continue along each bobble of the edge.

The seam becomes totally flat and invisible when completed.

Overtime

Overstitch is also known as oversewing or overcasting. It can be a bit fiddly, so before doing any sewing, it's a good idea to practise the stitch on a tension swatch or another old piece of knitting first.

Back Stitch

This is the most common stitch used to piece knitting together. Back stitch can be bulky and difficult for matching patterns as it is worked on the wrong side; however, it is a quick and strong stitch to use for designs in stocking stitch.

Always pin your work together before you start to stitch. Bring the yarn from the back to the front.

Insert the needle just behind where it last came out and bring it back through to the front just in front of where you started. Continue to work along the seam to the end.

Back Stitches

A back stitch seam is no good for a join that you want to have some give, but it is a solid technique and will hold your join tightly. It is best used for lightweight yarns because of its bulk. Beware when choosing your yarn, that this stitch may show through.

Knitting Off a Drop Sleeve

Knitting a drop sleeve to close a seam offers a tidier alternative to sewing one in. It can take a little time and practice to get this right, but the results are worth it. Follow the six simple steps below to create a garment with a clean and smooth finish.

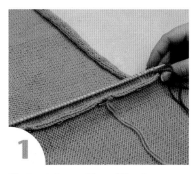

1 Work out the position of the sleeve as shown in Sewing a Drop Sleeve on page 56, then with right sides together safety pin into position.

2 Using a knitting needle and matching thread, pass the knitting needle through the body under the edge stitch and into the first stitch of the sleeve stitches.

3 Knit the stitch off the needle.

4 Bring the stitch through the side edge of the body.

5 Once you have two stitches on your RH needle, cast off the first stitch.

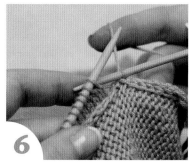

6 Continue across all the stitches.

Drop Shoulder Seams

Once main points have been pinned into place ease any excess between markers and pin securely. It's always best to tack into place with a contrasting yarn to avoid it moving. Remove the tacking once the seam is complete.

Sewing a Shallow Set-In Sleeve

Though a set-in sleeve may appear to have the simplest lines when you assemble it, the shaping can prove to be slightly more challenging than the drop sleeve. However, the result is much more slimming because the fabric doesn't bunch under the arm like that of a drop sleeve.

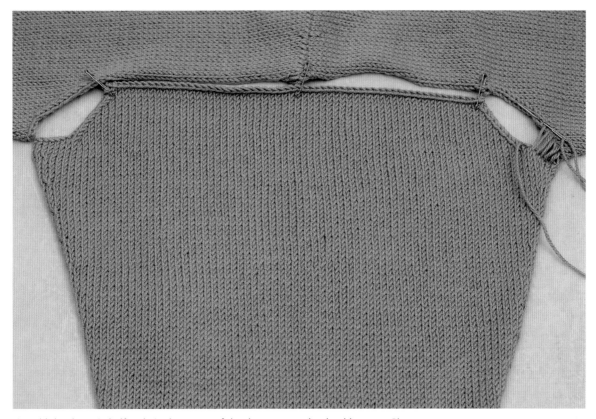

▲ Fold the sleeve in half and pin the centre of the sleeve top to the shoulder seam. Pin the armhole shaping as shown and mattress stitch into place as on page 54.

Ready, Set-In, GO!

In most cases a set-in sleeve can be sewn before the side seam in the body of the garment and before the sleeve seams. This will allow you to lay the project out on a table and see how evenly the easing has been done. Check your pattern directions to see if you should sew the seams first.

Set-In Sleeve

With this type of sleeve, you must first stitch the side seams of your sleeve and body. The body must be turned inside out, and the sleeve should be right side out.

Slip the sleeve into the armhole.

Matching the side seam to the sleeve seam, pin in place. Divide the top of the sleeve in half and at midpoint, and pin to the shoulder seam.

Pin the rest of the sleeve into place, matching the shaping.

Back stitch the sleeve into place (see page 57 for instructions).

Puffed Set-In Sleeve

Again with this type of sleeve, you must first stitch the side seams of your sleeve and body. The body must be turned inside out, and the sleeve should be right side out.

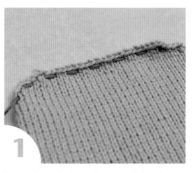

Run a thread along the top of the sleeve.

Tug each end to gather the top of the sleeve and secure in position.

Taking Care of Your Garments

After months of knitting and sewing, you need to take care of your precious garment and washing becomes a concern. Should it be washed by hand or in the machine? Should it be taken to the dry cleaner? Or should it be handed over to Mum? (I'm lucky, I have a mother who loves hand washing!)

Look at the ball band for the yarn and determine what is recommended. If it is machine washable, then it's best to put it in the machine. Hand washing can cause stretching and ruin shaping when the garment is full of water. It's always a good idea to wash your tension square in the way you would wash your garment.

Checking for bleeding of colour	If you would like to check if the dye will run in your yarn, take a sample of the yarn and wet it. Now wrap it round a piece of kitchen towel. You will see if the colour has run.
Hand washing	1. Don't wash your garment unless absolutely necessary. Sometimes they only need airing. Try hanging outside for the air to freshen it. 2. When you do wash your knits, use a gentle washing liquid (you will find a range of specialist hand wash products on the market) in tepid water and mix well before placing your garment in the water. 3. Gently wring the sweater while it is still immersed in the water. Never lift the garment out of the water as this will cause stretching. If you plan to wash your garment in a machine, I find it best to place in the machine on the rinse cycle. Avoid putting a single garment into the machine; add some towels if necessary. 4. Thoroughly rinse until the water runs clear. 5. Squeeze excess water from garment. Don't hang the garment out on the laundry line, since this will cause stretching. Lay flat if possible, but don't allow the garment to lay flat for too long in a wet condition. This will cause patching. 6. Try threading a pair of tights through the arms of the garment and hang on the line by the tights.
Machine washing	1. If the garment is machine washable, then place in the machine and wash at the required temperature. Never place it in the machine on its own – pack it out with towels if necessary. 2. Make sure to wash with the same sort of colours. 3. Always choose a short spin cycle as over spinning can cause felting. 4. Dry as in the hand washing section.
Dry cleaning	1. Make sure your dry cleaner knows exactly what type of fibre your garment is made from. 2. Make sure you air your garment when you get it back before you place it in your closet, as moths love the chemicals dry cleaners use. 3. Never store your garment in a plastic bag. 4. Always fold your garments rather than hang them. 5. Protect woollen garments from moths. Moths are attracted to dirt, oils and animal proteins. 6. If pressing a garment, always press on the wrong side and use a muslin cloth to protect it. 7. Keep spare yarn in case repairs are needed and also the ball band for details of washing.
Pilling	Some soft fibres, especially wool, may bobble after wear. Wool is just like your new wool carpet, sometimes it sheds and bobbles. This will happen in the first few times of wearing it. You can buy little machines that shave the bobbles off and make your garments look like new. After a few washes the pilling will calm down.

Lining a Jacket

If you have knitted a beautiful jacket, you may want to take the time to line it as this will help to keep it in shape. First, choose your lining. I encourage you to buy a lining at the same time as buying the yarn so you can find one in a matching colour. Use a good lightweight lining that will fold. Knitted fabric has a lot of movement, so choose something that is soft and will enhance the drape of your knitting.

Fabric Lining

Pin your knitted pieces onto the lining and cut out around each of them, allowing 2.5cm (1in) for a seam allowance. To gain extra movement in the body, allow 2.5cm (1in) extra across the width and make a pleat at the back of the neck.

Make your lining up in the same order as your knitted pieces. It's best to use a sewing machine to stitch them to give extra strength.

Slip the lining into the jacket, with the wrong side of the lining to the wrong side of the knitted jacket and pin into place.

Slip stitch the lining into the jacket with matching thread.

Knitted Lining

You may wish to consider a knitted lining. This works well when all the welts and sleeves are worked in double yarn – perhaps two strands of 4-ply – and the body is made in just single 4-ply yarn. When the garment is complete, knit another body in a contrasting 4-ply and slip stitch it into the body, wrong sides together, as a lining.

Pressing

Always check your ball band to see if the fibre can be pressed or not – what you do next will depend on the fibre composition of your yarn.

If your yarn can be pressed and the knitting is a smooth texture, stocking stitch for example, place a damp cloth onto your knitted pieces and press with a hot iron. Take care not to drag the iron across the work. Some people like to hold the steam iron approximately 10cm (4in) away from the fabric and just steam the pieces. If your yarn has mixed fibres, do not press. Instead, hold a steam iron fairly close to the surface and steam. If you have a fibre that cannot be pressed, then you may choose to spray the blocked pieces gently with cold water (using a spray like the ones for misting indoor plants), but do not saturate them. Press with a dry towel and your hands. Whichever technique you use, do not remove the pins until the pieces are dry. If you take them off the board while they are warm and damp, this may cause a lot of damage.

Alterations to Finished Garments

You have a garment that you absolutely love, but for whatever reason, the fit doesn't quite work. This chapter teaches you how to make easy alterations to create a gorgeous fit.

4

Making Adjustments

Once you have completed your garment, you may find that you are unhappy with the size. If the garment is too tight, you can unpick the seams and go back to your blocking board and try to gain some width with the use of steam and pinning. If you do this, you will lose some length. If your sweater is too wide, there really isn't anything you can do apart from unpicking the body and re-knitting it. Adding to or reducing the length isn't such a problem and there is a solution.

Adjusting the Length

The way knitting is structured, it is impossible to undo from the bottom of the work. To adjust the length without unpicking, you need to cut and rejoin your knitting. In the example, we are shortening a sleeve, but shortening the body follows the same principle.

Shortening the Sleeve

Measure how much you wish to lose and snip a bar between the stitches of that row.

Unpick along the row stitch by stitch.

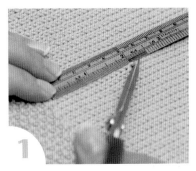

As you go, slip the stitches onto a knitting needle – it is best to use a circular needle.

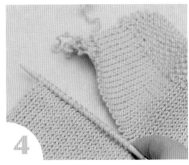

Once you have got to the end of the row, work in the other direction and continue in rib to match original.

The Long Run

In the same way that it is possible to shorten and remove stitching from a garment, it is also as simple to add length. To do so you should follow the same technique as shown on the left for shortening your work by cutting above the welt. The extra length would have to be added in the welt as it would show if you were to knit down in stocking stitch.

Necklines and Collars

A neckline can sometimes be the deciding factor as to whether you like a sweater or not and if you are going to make it. Many customers come up to me and say that they would love to make a particular sweater, but they don't like the high neck, or they would like to make their designs with a collar rather than a crew neck. Changing the neckline is relatively easy. Whether the sweater has a crew neck or a polo neck, the same neckline lies underneath. Here are some examples of what you can achieve by just knitting the actual neckband differently but keeping the neck shaping instructions exactly the same.

Crew Neck with Collar

▲ To be able to achieve this effect, pick up the stitches, beginning at centre front neck instead of as normal at left shoulder. Up right front, across the back and down the left front to the same centre point. Work backwards and forwards to length of collar required. Recommended length is 10cm (4in).

Cowl Neck

Crew Neck

▲ Here, the neckline is shown in a 2cm (¾in) rib. If your chosen pattern shows a polo neck that you don't like, pick up same amount of stitches but only knit to your desired length.

◀ This has been knitted in the same way as the polo neck, but this time the neckline is slightly wider. Casting off in knit will help the neck to lay flat onto the shoulders.

Polo Neck

▲ This neckline, once again, works on a normal crew neck sweater. Simply pick up and knit the stitches the pattern states and knit in chosen rib for approx 8cm (3¼in). Change needles to one size larger needle and continue in rib for a further 10cm (4in). Make sure you cast off loosely and in rib. For the best results, work on a circular needle so you don't get a seam.

Simple V-Neck

▲ The stitches have been picked up in the normal way and worked in four rows of St st, then bound off.

Beaded-Edge V-Neck

▲ The stitches have been picked up and then bound off. This is a useful edging for when you want a simple effect with a tidy edge.

Shawl Collar

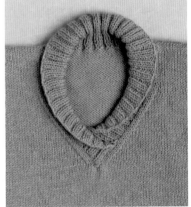

▲ To obtain this effect, start to pick up your stitches from the centre of the front V. Pick up left front across the back and down the right front, this time working backwards and forwards in your chosen rib for approx 8cm (3¼in). Cast off in rib.

Ribbed V-Neck

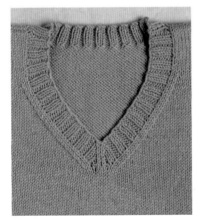

◀ To achieve this classic neckline, you have to mitre the centre stitches. In this example, I have chosen a k2, p2 rib. When you pick up your stitches, you must mark your centre of the V. Make sure the centre two stitches are worked in knit. At each side of the two centre stitches, you must decrease, by sloping to the left on the right-hand side of the centre and sloping to the right on the left-hand side of the V.

As described below:
Rib to 1 st before centre 2 sts, k2 tog, k2, skpo, rib to end.
Next row: Rib to 1 st before centre 2 sts, p2 tog tbl, p2, p2tog, rib to end.
Rep the last 2 rows twice more and the first row again.

Shoulder Pads

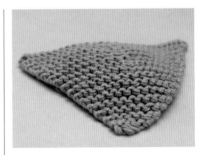

▲ Shoulder pads can improve the line of a jacket, but it is often impossible to find the right sort for the sweater or cardigan that you have just made. You need the right colour, the right size – and sometimes, it can be too much. However, you can make them in a yarn matching the garment and also in a size to suit it.

Garment Edging

An edging can be an effective way of altering an existing design, and they are fairly easy to do. To do this, knit the sweater and omit the welts. You then choose either an edging that is knitted lengthwise and slip stitched into place, or an edging that is picked up at the casted edge, knitted and then cast off again. There are a number of stitch reference books that specialise in edgings, but I have provided a few for you to try out. These pictures show the difference the edging can make.

▲ A basic silhouette has been adapted to create two classic designs. This scoopneck design boasts a decorative picot and a delicate lace trim. Plain yarns will enhance the detail of your edging more than textured ones.

▲ A ribbed edge lends a soft touch and adds extra elasticity to a garment. Play with variations of ribs to create your own desired effects.

Edgings Knitted Lengthwise

Beaded Edging

Cast on 5 sts.

Row 1: K5.

Row 2: K2, p1, k2.

Row 3: K1, PB, k1, m1, k2.

Row 4: K2, p2, k2.

Row 5: K3, m1, k3.

Row 6: K2, p3, k2.

Row 7: K1, PB, k1, m1, k4.

Row 8: K2, p4, k2.

Row 9: K3, m1, k5.

Row 10: K2, p5, k2.

Row 11: K1, PB, k1, m1, k6.

Row 12: K2, p6, k2.

Row 13: K3, m1, k7.

Row 14: K2, p7, k2.

Row 15: K1, PB, k1, m1, k8.

Row 16: K2, p8, k2.

Row 17: K2, sl 1, k1, psso, k8.

Row 18: K2, p7, k2.

Row 19: K1, PB, sl 1, K1, psso, k7.

Row 20: K2, p6, k2.

Row 21: K2, sl 1, k1, psso, k6.

Row 22: K2, p5, k2.

Row 23: K1, PB, sl 1, k1, psso, k5.

Row 24: K2, p4, k2.

Row 25: K2, sl 1, k1, psso, k4.

Row 26: K2, p3, k2.

Row 27: K1, PB, sl 1, k1, psso, k3.

Row 28: K2, p2, k2.

Row 29: K2, sl 1, k1, psso, k2.

Row 30: K2, p1, k2.

Cont to work from rows 3–30 until the trim is
the desired length.

Cast off.

Small Lacy Trim

Cast on 7 sts.

Row 1: K3, yfwd, k2togtbl, m2, k2.

Row 2: K3, p1, k2, yfwd, k2togtbl, k1tbl.

Row 3: K3, yfwd, k2tog tbl, k4.

Row 4: Cast off 2 sts, k4, yfwd, k2tog tbl, k1tbl.

Rep rows 1–4 until the trim is the desired length.

Cast off.

Cable Edging

Cast on 20 sts.

Row 1: K3, p17.

Row 2: K20.

Row 3: K3, p17.

Row 4: K20.

Row 5: K3, p17.

Row 6: K1, c8b, k3.

Rows 7–12: Work rows 1 & 2 three times more.

Row 13: Work as for row 1.

Row 14: Work as for row 6.

Repeat from row 7–14 until the trim is the desired length.

Cast off.

Lace diamond

Cast on 9 sts.

Row 1: Sl 1, k2, m1, k2tog, k1, m2, k2tog, k1.

Row 2: K3, p1, k3, m1, k2tog, k1.

Row 3: Sl 1, k2, m1, k2tog, k5.

Row 4: K7, m1, k2tog, k1.

Row 5: Sl 1, k2, m1, k2tog, k1, m2, k2tog, m2, k2.

Row 6: K3, p1, k2, p1, k3, m1, k2tog, k1.

Row 7: Sl 1, k2, m1, k2tog, k8.

Row 8: K10, m1, k2tog, k1.

Row 9: Sl 1, k2, m1, k2tog, k1, m2, k2tog, m2, k2tog, m2, k2tog, k1.

Row 10: K3, p1, k2, p1, k2, p1, k3, m1, k2tog, k1.

Row 11: Sl 1, k2, m1, k2tog, k11.

Row 12: Cast off 7 sts, k5, m1, k2tog, k1.

Repeat rows 1–12 until the trim is the desired length.

Cast off.

Large Lacy Trim

Cast on 11 sts.

Row 1: K4, yrn, p2tog, k4, yfwd, (k1, p1) into last st.

Row 2: K3, yrn, p2tog, k4, yrn, p2tog, k1, sl 1.

Row 3: K4, yrn, p2tog, k1, p2tog, yon, k4.

Row 4: K5, yrn, p2tog, k2, yrn, p2tog, k1, sl 1.

Row 5: K4, yrn, p2tog, k2, yrn, p2tog, k3.

Row 6: Cast off 3 sts, yfwd, k5, yrn, p2tog, k1, sl 1.

Repeat rows 1–6 until the trim is the desired length.

Cast off.

Fringed Trim

Cast on 20 sts.

Row 1: Knit.

Row 2: Knit.

Row 3: Cast off 17 sts, k3.

Row 4: K3, turn, cast on 17 sts.

Row 5: Knit.

Row 6: Knit.

Row 7: As row 3.

Repeat rows 4–7 until the trim is the desired length.

Cast off.

Edgings Picked Up and Knitted

Beaded Edging

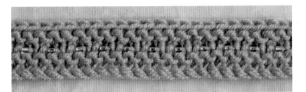

To work this edging, you need to have a total number of stitches that is divisible by two, plus two extra. You can choose to pick up the lower edge of a piece of knitting and work down, or alternatively, you can cast on and work the edging, then move onto the main stitch for your garment.

Cast on required amount of sts.
Row 1: Knit.
Row 2: Knit.
Row 3: (K1, PB), to end.
Row 4: Knit.
Row 5: Knit.
Cast off.

Knitted Picot

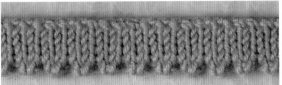

This edging requires you to pick up and knit, or cast on, a total number of stitches that is divisible by two, plus two extra.

Cast on required amount of sts.
Work 4 rows in St st.
Next Row: (K2 tog, yfwd twice) to end of row.
Work 4 rows in St st.
Cast off.

Scallop

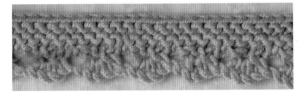

To make this edging, you need to pick up and knit, or cast on, a total number of stitches that is divisible by five, plus two extra.

Cast on required amount of sts.
Row 1: K1, yfwd and over needle to make one stitch, *K5, turn, lift 2nd, 3rd, 4th & 5th sts over the first st and off the needle, turn, yfwd* Repeat from * to * to end.
Row 2: K1, *(p1, yon to make one st, k1 tbl) all into next st, p1, repeat from * to end.
Row 3: K2, k1 tbl, *k3, k1 tbl*, repeat from * to * to last 2 sts, k2.
Work 3 rows garter st.
Cast off.

On Edge

A carefully thought out and well-designed edging can really make a garment so it is important to thoroughly consider all the details ensuring that it will not only work but look great too. When choosing an edging, consider the depth of the edging itself. Will it take your garment to the overall length you require it to be? If it is shallower than the edging suggested in the pattern, make sure you have increased the main body length to compensate. Use a smaller needle to knit your edging than the main body.

Frill Edging

This frill must either be made first before starting your garment, or cast off and stitched into place. To calculate how many stitches you need to do this edging, you need four times more than the actual number on the edge you are attaching it to.

Cast on required amount of sts.
Work 4 rows St st.
Next row: (K2tog) across row. (150 sts)
Work a further 3 rows in St st.
Next row: (K2tog) across row. (75 sts)
Hold these sts on a spare needle.

Work a second frill using the same amount of sts but this time:
Work 6 rows St st.
Next row: (K2tog) across row. (150 sts)
Work a further 3 rows in St st.
Join the two frills together as folls:
Lay the first frill on top of the second frill, now knit together one stitch from the first frill and one stitch from the second frill. Continue like this across all the sts.

Bobble Trim

To work this edge, you need to pick up and knit, or cast on, a total number of stitches that is divisible by five, plus two extra.

Work 5 rows seed stitch.
Cast off bobble row: Cast off 4, * MB, cast off 4, rep from * to end.

MB: Make bobble – Knit into front, back, front, back and front of the next stitch.
1. Slip all five stitches back onto LH needle, then knit them.
2. Slip all five stitches back onto LH needle, then knit them.
3. Now pass each stitch over the last stitch knitted until you are back to one stitch.

Frill Seeker

Edgings are guaranteed to add a bit of fun to a project. Don't be afraid to experiment and create something new. If you're not feeling confident, then make a simple change to an established design. You could work this frill the other way up if you wish, by reversing the shapings to increase in every stitch rather than decrease.

Crochet Edgings

There isn't anything more annoying than falling in love with a design and finding out that the edging is crocheted, especially when you don't know how to crochet. First of all, go and learn – admittedly, I wasn't a lover of crochet, but I picked it up a couple of years ago and haven't looked back since. It makes edgings really quick and simple, and now I actually enjoy the motion of crochet. If you can't face the thought of learning something new, the edgings below will give you a similar look to crochet.

Beaded Edging

This is a simple alternative when the pattern says finish raw edges with double crochet. Simply pick up the stitches along the raw edge, turn and cast off.

Casted Off Picot

Pick up your stitches along the raw edge, and knit 1 row. (You may choose to do more rows before you cast off.)

Cast off picot row: (Cast off 3 sts, cast on 2 sts in the stitch on your LH needle, cast off the 2 sts.) Repeat across the row until 1 st remains. Fasten off.

Scallop Trim

Cast on multiples of eight, plus two, for the required length of edging.

Row 1: Purl.
Row 2: K2, *k1, sl this st back onto LH needle then lift the next 8 sts on LH needle over this st and off the needle, yfwd twice, then knit st on LH needle again, k2*, repeat from * to * to end.
Row 3: K1, *p2tog, (k1, K1tbl) into double yfwd of previous row, p1*, repeat from * to * to last st, k1.
Row 4: Knit.
Cast off.

Scallop Lace Trim

Cast on multiples of eight, plus two, for the required length of edging.

Row 1: Purl.
Row 2: K2, *k1, sl this st back onto LH needle then lift the next 5 sts on LH needle over this st and off the needle, m2, then k the first st again, k2*, repeat from * to * to end.
Row 3: K1, *p2tog, drop extra loop of 2 sts made on previous row and into this loop (k1, K1tbl) twice, p1*, repeat from * to * to last st, k1.
Work 5 rows garter stitch.
Cast off.

Embellishments

Accenting garments and accessories with
embellishments such as beading, sequins
or pompoms can be one of the most
rewarding aspects of knitting as the results
range from playful and whimsical to
elegant and sophisticated.

5

Beading

Beading is always fun to do and even the most basic designs can be transformed with a row of beading around the cuff or edge of a collar. They not only add a bit of glamour, but can be used to easily accentuate detail in a pattern. Beads can only be placed every alternate stitch and row, as demonstrated in the steps, but they can be placed on a purl row in the same way.

Beaded Knitting

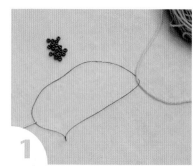

1 Use sewing thread or yarn.

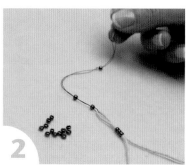

2 Thread the beads onto the thread.

3 Bring the yarn forward and slip the bead down tight in front of the work.

4 Slip the next stitch purlwise.

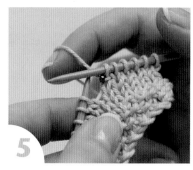

5 Take the yarn to the back of the work.

6 Knit the next stitch quite tightly.

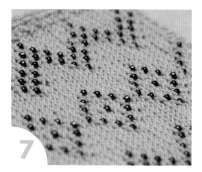

7 This is how the finished work should look.

Add a Bit of Sparkle

As an alternative to beading, when used sparingly, the addition of sequins will add instant glamour to any project. They can be placed on the yarn and knitted exactly the same way as beads or try sewing them on carefully once the project is complete.

Fringing

Fringing makes a nice and easy finish for garments, accessories and home accents. Try making beaded fringes or knotting fringes together in alternate rows for striking results. The most simple and commonly used fringing is described below, but try using a variety of colours and knot the yarn together in different ways to create inspirational textures and effects.

Plain Fringing

1 Thread the needle with yarn for the fringe and bring through the lower edge of work.

2 Slip knot into place.

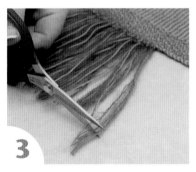

3 Trim to the correct length.

4 This is how the finished work should look.

Fringe Benefits

When you have made your fringe, you could always try plaiting three or more tassles together for a different and interesting effect.

Alternatively, divide each tassle in half and knot each half to the adjacent tassle. This will result in a more complex detail which will look attractive on the edge of any garment.

Remember to trim the yarn carefully when evening out the yarn lengths. But don't worry, you can always remove one or two and try again.

Beaded Fringing

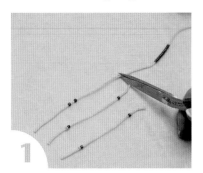

1 Thread the beads onto the yarn as shown on page 78. Cut the yarn to the lengths required, with two beads on each length, allowing a little extra for knotting. Knot each end to stop the beads from escaping.

2 Thread the yarn onto the needle and bring through the edge of the work.

3 Slip knot into place and trim to match.

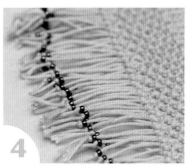

4 This is how the finished work should look.

Bead It

Sourcing beads can be difficult, but exciting as well. Knitting bead sizes should be 3mm ($\frac{1}{8}$in) or 4mm ($\frac{3}{16}$in) and I always recommend glass beads because they are washable. During my travels, I have found beautiful bead shops in London, Paris, Amsterdam and especially New York, where an entire street is devoted to them.

If you haven't got a bead haven near you, there are an enormous number of bead retailers that can be found on the internet or that trade by mail order.

Knitted Fringing

This is made in one piece and stitched onto the work.

Cast on 3 sts and knit them.

Row 1: P3, turn and cast on 14 sts.

Row 2: Cast off 14 sts, k2, turn.

Row 3: Cast off 2 sts purlwise, p2, turn and cast on 14 sts.

Row 4: As row 2.

Repeat these last 2 rows until fringe is as long as needed.

Pompoms

There are some great pompom makers available on the market, which makes pompoms incredibly easy to make. If you don't want to use one, then cut two circles from pieces of cardboard and make a large hole in the middle. You then thread the yarn around the circles until the hole in the middle is full and follow from step 3 below.

Creating a Pompom

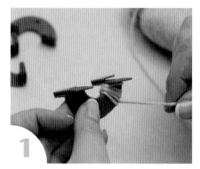

1. Using a pompom maker, wrap the yarn around each half.

2. Join the two halves together.

3. Cut around the centre of the pompom.

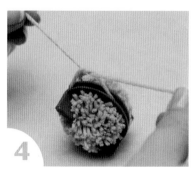

4. Tie a length of yarn around the centre.

5. Remove the plastic parts of the pompom maker (or the cardboard rings, if you are using these).

6. The finished pompom will look like this.

Tassels

Tassels are a cinch to create and if you make your own, you can use the same yarn the garment is made in so they will match exactly. Alternatively, you can be as creative as you like with your yarn colour selection and choose colours that will have a dramatic effect on the finished project.

Making Tassels

1

Wrap the chosen yarn around a piece of cardboard the same length as your desired length of tassel.

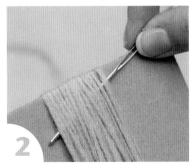

2

Cut another length of yarn and thread through top, securing with a knot.

3

Cut through the loops at the lower edge of the tassel.

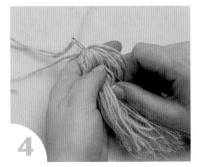

4

Take one end of the yarn at the top and thread it through to where you wish your tassel to be tied.

5

Wrap the length around the tassel several times and secure.

6

Trim the ends and the tassel is finished.

Hanging In

Though tassels can often be made as accents on pillows and other home furnishings, they can create decorative ends for ties of outerwear such as ponchos and capes.

Cords and Braids

When making a braid, try mixing different types of yarn to alter the finished effect. In the cords on page 86, I've added a fine lurex to soft cashmere and very fine kid silk to achieve some unique results. This can be done with almost any yarn and in the colours of your choice.

I-Cord

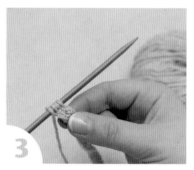

Using double-pointed needles, cast on two stitches and increase to four stitches on the first row. Knit the four stitches.

The stitches will now be at end of the RH needle.

Do not turn; push the stitches to the other end of needle. Repeat the process until the cord is the desired length.

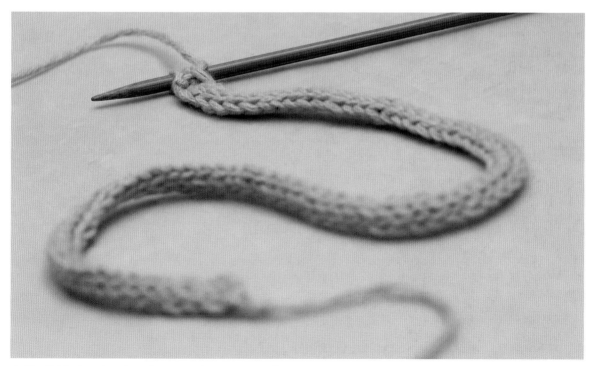

▲ The finished cord can be as long or as short as you need.

Braided Cord

1

2

Pin down three strands of yarn and divide them into left, centre and right. Move right over centre, then left over centre. Alternate as set until the braid is the desired length.

This is how the finished cord should look.

Twisted Cord

1

2

Take two strands of yarn and knot them together at one end, then secure the end in place (try a door handle). Twist the cord until it is tight.

Loose the fixed end and let the cord twist upon itself.

3

4

Tighten the second twist and secure the ends.

This is how the finished cord should look.

French Knitting

You may remember doing this as a child and it was possibly your first attempt at knitting. For French knitting, you need a 'dolly', but you can make one with a thread reel and four nails – if you can find a wooden thread reel! French knitting is a useful embellishment that can be used to make handles for knitted bags.

Basic Cord

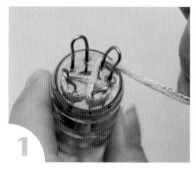

1

To thread the dolly, push the end of the yarn through the centre and wrap it around each pin in an anti-clockwise direction.

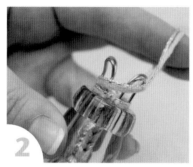

2

Wrap the yarn around a pin.

3

Pick up the stitch below.

4

Place over the yarn and pin, then continue in a counterclockwise direction.

5

This is how the finished cord should look.

Basic Training

Make sure that you keep the yarn taut while creating the basic cord. This will ensure a consistency of stitch size and neat finish giving you the desired professional look.

Knitted Braid

Use any yarn of your choice and a knitting needle to match your ply. For instance, if you are using 2 x DK weights, this makes a chunky weight and I would use a 5.5mm (US 9) needle. To work out how many stitches to cast on, make a tension swatch and calculate how many stitches to the inch.

Cast on 88 sts, then cast them off fairly loosely. Pull the cord out to its full length.

Lace Braid

Use any yarn of your choice (see the notes for Knitted Braid on the left).

Cast on 2 sts.

Row 1: Yon to back, sl 1 purlwise, k1, psso.

NB: Take care not to confuse the strand of the 'yon' with the 'Sl 1, k1, psso'.

Continue to work until you've reached the desired length. Cast off.

Embroidery

The best use of this stitch is for outlining designs, whether it be a motif or a monogram. There are countless stitch types, so here I've included some of the most popular ones.

Stem Stitch

Stem stitch is one of the most popular outlining stitches. If a thicker stem stitch is required for a design, make the angle at which the stitch is taken greater.

Bring the needle through from the back of the work, insert it back into the fabric from right to left at a slight angle. Repeat close together as shown.

Blanket Stitch

This stitch is ideal for edging a raw knitted edge and it stops the edge from curling up. As its name suggests, it was mostly used for edging blankets.

Working from left to right, bring the needle through the piece of fabric from the back, insert the needle back into the fabric from the front, catch the loop of yarn around the needle and pull into place.

Chain Stitch

Chain stitch is a decorative stitch worked in a line. Bring the needle through from the back.

Insert the needle back into the same hole, then out again a short distance away along the line you are sewing, looping the yarn around the tip of needle in order to make the chain.

Lazy Daisy

This can be used to make a decorative flower embellishment without too much work.

Make a chain stitch as described above, but place the chains in a circle as shown. Sew a small stitch at the end of the chain to secure it in place.

Bullion Stitch

This decorative stitch lends a 3-D look to your work. Bring the needle through to the front from the back of the fabric. Insert the needle back into the fabric and out again, without pulling the needle completely out. Wrap the yarn around the needle five times. Hold the yarn firmly and pull the needle free of the fabric, pull tight, then take your needle through to the back of the fabric and fasten off.

French Knots

This 3-D stitch provides textural interest to your work. Bring the needle through from the back of the fabric. Wrap the yarn around the needle three times. Hold the yarn firmly and insert the needle back into the same space from where it came and fasten off.

Swiss Darning

Swiss darning resembles a knit stitch and can be used for adding colour detail without all the fuss of knitting with several colours. It may also be used to hide a mistake in your knitting.

Bring the needle through from the back of the fabric at the base of a knitted stitch, then insert the needle at the top of the stitch going from right to left.

Insert the needle back into the original space at the bottom of the stitch and your stitch is complete.

Needle Arts

Avoid using old embroidery needles as they will cause inconsistent embroidery and breaks. Try to change your needle regularly if you do a lot of embroidering.

Corsages

Corsages always dress up a garment and they're deceptively easy to knit. The choice of yarn makes a huge difference to a corsage, so try the same pattern again in a different type of yarn and see what happens.

Decorative Twirl

▲ This corsage uses techniques that can be found in Short Row Shaping on page 31.

Cast on 50 sts and work 4 rows in St st.

Row 5: Inc 1 into next 10 sts, knit to end.

Row 6: Purl 40 sts, wrap st and turn.

Row 7: Inc 1 in next 14 sts, knit to end.

Row 8: Purl 26 sts, wrap st and turn.

Row 9: Inc 1 in next to end.

Row 10: Work one row across all sts picking up wrapped stitches.

Row 11: Knit one row in contrast yarn.

Cast off.

Roll the fabric around itself and stitch into place.

Sew some beads into the centre of the flower.

Sea Anemone

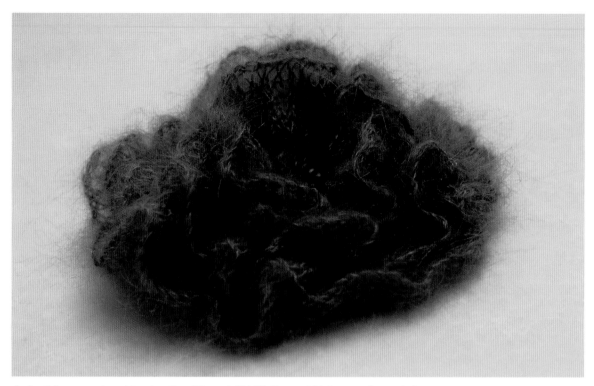

▲ For this corsage, I used two lengths of Rowan's Kid Silk Haze, which is a very fine mohair.

Cast on 250 sts.
Work 4 rows St st.
Next row: (K2tog) across row. (150 sts)
Work a further 3 rows in St st.
Next row: (K2tog) across row. (75 sts)
Hold these sts on a spare needle.
Work a second frill using the same
amount of sts but this time working:
Work 6 rows St st.
Next row: (K2tog) across row. (150 sts)
Work a further 5 rows in St st.

Next row: (K2tog) across row. (75 sts)
Join the two frills together as folls:
Lay the first frill on top of the second
frill, now knit together one stitch from
the first frill and one stitch from the
second frill. Work like this across all sts.
Do not cast off. Thread the yarn
through the stitches and gather. Stitch
into place and add beads to the centre.

Elegant Rose

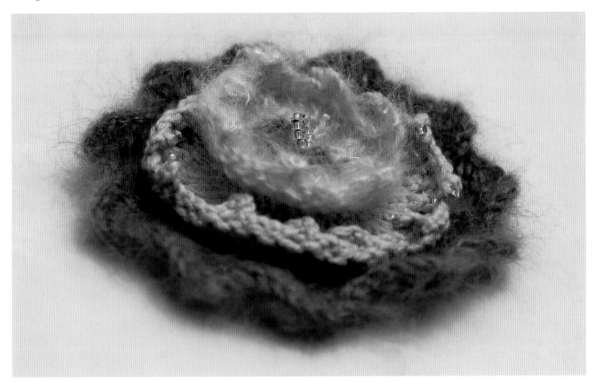

▲ I used a combination of yarns to create the delicate effect of this corsage.

Centre petal

Cast on 11 sts and knit 1 row.

Next row: Inc one st in every st.

Work 3 rows in St st.

Next row: (K2tog, yfwd) to end of row.

Purl 1 row.

Foll row: (PB, k1) to end.

Cast off as follows: *Cast off 3 sts, Cast on 2 sts in the stitch on your LH needle, cast off 2 sts rep from * across row.

Fasten off.

Middle petal

Cast on 22 sts and knit 1 row.

Next row: Inc one st in every st.

Work 3 rows in St st.

Next row: (K2tog, yfwd) to end of row.

Purl 1 row.

Foll row: (PB, k1) to end.

Cast off as follows: *Cast off 3 sts, Cast on 2 sts in the stitch on your LH needle, cast off 1st, placing bead at the same time, cast off another st and repeat from * across row.

Fasten off.

Outer petal

Cast on 110 sts and knit 1 row.

Row 2: K2, *k1, sl this st back onto LH needle then lift the next 8 sts on LH needle over this st and off the needle, yfwd twice, then knit st on LH needle again, k2*, repeat from * to * to end.

Row 3: K1, *p2tog, (k1, K1tbl) into double yfwd of previous row, p1*, repeat from * to * to last st, k1.

Row 4: Knit.

Next row: (K2tog, k2) to end.

Work 4 rows in St st.

Next row: (K2tog, k1) to end.

Work 2 rows in St st.

Placing the middle petal on top of the work on the needle, pick up and knit stitches together with the yarn used for the outer petal.

Purl 1 row.

Place centre petal on top of the work and pick up one centre petal stitch and work together with two stitches from the needle.

Knit 1 row.

Cut yarn and thread through the stitches, gather up and fasten off.

Patterns

From a basic pullover to a
button-front cardigan to a stylish
evening bag, these projects are
designed to inspire and incorporate
many of the techniques found
throughout the book.

Lace-Edged Pullover

MATERIALS

6(7:7:8:8:9) balls of Calmer by Rowan in Powder Puff, 160m/50g, 75% cotton/25% acrylic/microfibre
Pair of 4mm (US 6) and 5mm (US 8) knitting needles.

MEASUREMENTS

To fit bust:

81	86	92	97	102	107	cm
32	34	36	38	40	42	in

Actual measurements

Bust

92	98	103	108	114	121	cm
36¼	38½	40½	42½	45	47½	in

Length to shoulder

53	54	55	56	57	58	cm
21	21¼	21¾	22	22½	23	in

Sleeve length

43	43	44	44	45	45	cm
17	17	17¼	17¼	17¾	17¾	in

TENSION

21 sts and 30 rows to 10cm (4in) square over St st on 5mm (US 8) needles.

ABBREVIATIONS

See page 109.

BACK

With 5mm (US 8) needles, cast on 100(106:112:118:124:130) sts.
Beg with a knit row cont in St st.
Work 2 rows.
Dec row: K5, skpo, k to last 7 sts, k2 tog, k5.
Work 5 rows.
Rep the last 6 rows 5 times more and the dec row again 86 (92:98:104:110:116) sts.
Cont straight until back measures 6cm (6¼in) from cast on edge, ending with a wrong side row.
Inc row: K3, m1, k to last 3 sts, m1, k3.
Work 5 rows.
Rep the last 6 rows three times more and the inc row again.

96(102:108:114:120:126) sts.
Cont straight until Back measures 30(30:31:31:32:32)cm (11¾[11¾:12¼:12¼:12½:12½]in) from cast on edge, ending with a wrong side row.
Shape armholes
Cast off 5(5:6:6:7:7) sts at beg of next 2 rows.
Dec one st at each end of next and every foll alt row until 76(80:82:84:88:92) sts rem.
Cont in St st until back measures 47(48:49:50:51:52)cm (18½[19:19¼:19¾:20:20½]in) from cast on edge, ending with a wrong side row.
Shape neck
Next row: K19(20:21:22:23:24) sts, turn and work on these sts for first side of neck shaping.
Dec one st at neck edge on next 4 rows 15(16:17:18:19:20) sts.
Work 1 row.
Shape shoulder
Cast off 7(7:8:8:9:9) sts at beg of next row.
Work 1 row.
Cast off rem 8(9:9:10:10:11) sts.
With right side facing, slip centre 38(40:40:42:42:44) sts onto a spare needle, rejoin yarn to rem sts, k to end.
Complete to match first side of neck shaping.
Dec one st at neck edge on next 4 rows. 15(16:17:18:19:20) sts.
Work 2 rows.

FRONT

Work as given for back until front measures 41(42:43:44:45:46)cm (16[16½:17:17¼:17½:18]in) from cast on edge, ending with a wrong side row.
Shape neck
Next row: K24(25:26:27:28:29) sts, turn and work on these sts for first side of neck shaping.
Dec one st at neck edge on next 9 rows. 15(16:17:18:19:20) sts.
Work straight until front matches back to shoulder, ending at armhole edge.

Shape shoulder

Cast off 7(7:8:8:9:9) sts at beg of next row.

Work 1 row.

Cast off rem 8 (9:9:10:10:11) sts.

With right side facing, slip centre 28(30:30:32:32:34) sts onto a spare needle, rejoin yarn to rem sts, k to end.

Dec one st at neck edge on next 9 rows. 16(17:18:19:20:21) sts.

Work straight until front matches back to shoulder, ending at armhole edge.

Cast off 7(7:8:8:9:9) sts at beg of next row.

Work 1 row.

Cast off rem 8(9:9:10:10:11) sts.

SLEEVES

With 5mm (US 8) needles, cast on 44(46:48:52:54:56) sts.

Beg with a k row, cont in St st.

Work 4 rows.

Inc row: K3, m1, k to last 3 sts, m1, k3.

Work 9 rows.

Rep the last 10 rows until there are 66(68:70:74:76:78) sts.

Cont straight until Sleeve measures 39(39:40:40:41:41)cm (15¼[15¼:15¾:15¾:16:16]in) from cast on edge, ending with a purl row.

Shape sleeve top

Cast off 5(5:6:6:7:7) sts at beg of next 2 rows.

Dec 1 st at each end of the next 3 rows then 3 foll alt rows then every foll 4th row until 34(34:36:36:38:38) sts rem. then on every foll alt row until 30 sts rem.

Cast off 3 sts at beg of next 2 rows.

Cast off.

NECK EDGING

Join right shoulder seam.

With right side facing, using 4mm (US 6) needles, pick up and k22 sts down left side of front neck, k28(30:30:32:32:34) sts from front neck holder, pick up and k22 sts up right side of front neck, 8 sts down right back neck, k across

38(40:40:42:42:44) sts from back neck holder, pick up and k8 sts up right side of back neck.126(130:130:134:134:138) sts.

Next row: P to end.

Next row: (picot row) K1, * k2 tog, y2rn; rep from * to last st, k1.

Next row: P to end, purling once into y2rn.

Next row: K to end.

CUFF EDGINGS

With right side facing, using 4mm (US 6) needles, pick up and k44(46:48:52:54:56) sts along cast on edge of sleeve.

Work as given for neck edging.

LOWER EDGING

With 5mm (US 8) needles, cast on 9 sts.

Row 1: Sl 1, k2, yf, k2 tog, k1, y2rn, k2 tog, k1.

Row 2: K3, p1, k3, yf, k2 tog, k1.

Row 3: Sl 1, k2, yf, k2 tog, k5.

Row 4: K7, yf, k2 tog, k1.

Row 5: Sl 1, k2, yf, k2 tog, k1, y2rn, k2 tog, y2rn, k2.

Row 6: K3, p1, k2, p1, k3, yf, k2 tog, k1.

Row 7: Sl 1, k2, yf, k2 tog, k8.

Row 8: K10, yf, k2 tog, k1.

Row 9: Sl 1, k2, yf, k2 tog, k1, [y2rn, k2 tog] 3 times, k1.

Row 10: K3, p1, k2, p1, k2, p1, k3, yf, k2 tog, k1.

Row 11: Sl 1, k2, yf, k2 tog, k11.

Row 12: Cast off 7 sts, k next 5 sts, yf, k2 tog, k1.

These 12 rows form the patt.

Cont in patt until edging fits along lower edge of pullover, ending row 12.

Cast off.

TO FINISH

Join left shoulder and neck edging seam. Sew on sleeves. Join side and sleeve seams.

Fold neck and sleeve edgings to wrong side along picot row and slip stitch in place. Join short ends of lower edging and sew in place.

Easy-Fit Sweaters

MATERIALS

8(9:9:10:11:11) balls of Wool Cotton by Rowan in August, 113m/50gm, 50% wool/50% cotton Or 5(6:6:6:7:7) balls of Felted Tweed by Rowan in Bilberry, 175m/50g, 50% wool/25% alpaca/25% rayon
Pair of 3¼mm (US 4) and 4mm (US 6) knitting needles.

MEASUREMENTS

To fit bust:

81	86	92	97	102	107	cm
32	34	36	38	40	42	in

Actual measurements
Bust

92	98	103	108	114	120	cm
36¼	38½	40½	42½	45	47¼	in

Length to shoulder

53	54	55	56	57	58	cm
21	21¼	21¾	22	22½	23	in

Sleeve length

43	43	44	44	45	45	cm
17	17	17¼	17¼	17¾	17¾	in

TENSION

22 sts and 30 rows to 10cm (4in) square over St st on 4mm (US 6) needles.

ABBREVIATIONS

See page 109.

BACK

Cast on 102(110:114:122:126:134) sts using 3¼mm (US 3) needles.
Row 1: K2, * p2, k2; rep from * to end.
Row 2: P2, * k2, p2; rep from * to end.
Rep the last 2 rows once more, increasing 2 sts evenly across last row on **1st, 3rd and 5th sizes only**.
104(110:116:122:128:134) sts.
Change to 4mm (US 6) needles.
Beg with a k row cont in St st.
Work 8 rows.
Dec row: K6, skpo, k to last 8 sts, k2tog, k6.

Work 5 rows.
Rep the last 6 rows 5 times more and the dec row again.
90(96:102:108:114:120) sts.
Cont straight until back measures 20cm (8in) from cast on edge, ending with a wrong side row.
Inc row: K3, m1, k to last 3 sts, m1, k3.
Work 5 rows.
Rep the last 6 rows 3 times more and the inc row again.
100(106:112:118:124:130) sts.
Cont straight until Back measures 34(34:35:35:36:36)cm (13½[13½:13¾:13¾:14¼:14¼]in) from cast on edge, ending with a wrong side row.

Shape armholes

Cast off 5(5:6:6:7:7) sts at beg of next 2 rows.
Dec one st at each end of next and every foll alt row until 80(84:86:88:92:96) sts rem.
Cont in St st until back measures 51(52:53:54:55:56)cm (20[20½:21:21¼:21¾:22]in) from cast on edge, ending with a wrong side row.

Shape neck

Next row: K20(21:22:23:24:25) sts, turn and work on these sts for first side of neck shaping.
Next row: Cast off 2 sts, p to end.
Next row: K to end.
Rep the last 2 rows once more.
16 (17:18:19:20:21) sts.
P 1 row.

Shape shoulder

Next row: K to end.
Next row: P to last 8(8:9:9:10:10) sts, turn.
Next row: Sl 1, k to end.
Leave all sts on a stitch holder.
With right side facing, slip centre 40(42:42:44:44:46) sts onto a holder, rejoin yarn to rem sts, k to end.
Next row: P to end.
Next row: Cast off 2 sts, k to end.
Rep the last 2 rows once more.
16(17:18:19:20:21) sts.
P 1 row.

Next row: K to last 8(8:9:9:10:10) sts, turn.
Next row: Sl 1, p to end.
Leave all sts on a stitch holder.

FRONT

Work as given for back until front measures 48(49:50:51:52:53)cm (19[19¼:19¾:20:20½:21]in) from cast on edge, ending with a wrong side row.

Shape neck

Next row: K25(26:27:28:29:30) sts, turn and work on these sts for first side of neck shaping.
Next row: P2, p2tog, p to end.
Next row: K to last 4 sts, k2tog, k2.
Rep the last 2 rows 3 times more and the first row again. 16(17:18:19:20:21) sts.
Work a few rows straight until front measures same as Back to shoulder shaping, ending at armhole edge.

Shape shoulder

Next row: K to end.
Next row: P to last 8(8:9:9:10:10) sts, turn.
Next row: Sl 1, k to end.
Leave all sts on a stitch holder.
With right side facing, slip centre 30(32:32:34:34:36) sts onto a holder, rejoin yarn to rem sts, K to end.
Next row: P to last 4 sts p2tog tbl, p2.
Next row: K2, skpo, k to end.
Rep the last 2 rows 3 times more and the first row again. 16(17:18:19:20:21) sts.
Work a few rows straight until front measures same as Back to shoulder shaping, ending at armhole edge.
Next row: K to last 8 (8:9:9:10:10) sts, turn.
Next row: Sl 1, p to end.
Leave all sts on a stitch holder.

SLEEVES

With 3¼ mm (US 3) needles, cast on 42(46:50:54:58:62) sts.
Work 8 rows rib as given for Back.
Change to 4mm (US 6) needles.
Beg with a k row, cont in St st.

Work 4 rows.
Inc row: K3, m1, k to last 3 sts, m1, k3.
Work 5 rows.
Rep the last 6 rows until there are 80(84:88:92:96:100) sts.
Cont straight until Sleeve measures 43(43:44:44:45:45)cm (17[17:17¼:17¼:17¾:17¾]in) from cast on edge, ending with a p row.

Shape sleeve top

Cast off 5(5:6:6:7:7) sts at beg of next 2 rows.
Dec 1 st at each end of the next row and 4(5:6:8:8:9) foll alt rows.
P 1 row.
Cast off rem 60(62:62:62:64:66) sts.

COLLAR

Join right shoulder as follows:
With point of needles facing neck edges, place sts from left back shoulder and left front shoulder each on a 4mm (US 6) needle, with the right side of back and front together, using a third 4mm (US 6) needle, knit the first st from each needle together, then knit the second st from each needle together, pass the first stitch over the second stitch and off the needle, knit the third st from each needle together, pass the second stitch over the third stitch and off the needle, cont in this way until all the stitches have been casted off.
With right side facing and 3¼mm (US 3) needles, pick up and k19 sts down left side of front neck, k across 30(32:32:34:34:36) sts from centre front holder, pick up and k19 sts up right side of front neck, 19 sts down right side of back neck, k across 40(42:42:44:44:46) sts from back neck holder, pick up and k11 sts up left side of back neck. 130(134:134:138:138:142) sts.
Row 1: P2, * k2, p2; rep from * to end.
Row 2: K2, * p2, k2; rep from * to end.
Rep the last 2 rows until collar measures 6cm (2½ in).
Cast off in rib.

TO FINISH

Join left shoulder seam in the same way as right shoulder, then join collar seam. Sew on sleeves. Join side and sleeve seams.

Lined Jacket

MATERIALS

7(8:8:7:7:8) balls of Summer Tweed by Rowan in Cape (M). 108m/50g, 70% silk/30% cotton
2 balls of All Seasons Cotton by Rowan in Jazz (C). 90m/50g, 60% cotton/40% acrylic/microfibre
Pair of 4¼mm (US 7) and 5mm (US 8) knitting needles.
7 Buttons

MEASUREMENTS

To fit bust:

81	86	92	97	102	107	cm
32	34	36	38	40	42	in

Actual measurements

Bust

95	100	105	110	115	120	cm
37½	39½	41½	43½	45¼	47¼	in

Length to shoulder

52	53	54	55	56	57	cm
20½	21	21¼	21¾	22	22½	in

Sleeve length

43	43	44	44	45	45	cm
17	17	17¼	17¼	17¾	17¾	in

TENSION

16 sts and 23 rows to 10cm (4in) square over St st using 5mm (US 8) needles and Summer Tweed.
17 sts and 24 rows to 10cm (4in) square over St st using 5mm (US 8) needles and All Seasons Cotton.

ABBREVIATIONS

See page 109.

BACK

With 5mm (US 8) needles and M cast on 78(82:86:90:94:98) sts.
Beg with a k row cont in St st until back measures 35(35:36:36:37:37)cm (13¾[13¾:14¼:14¼:14½:14½]in) from cast on edge, ending with a wrong side row.

Shape armholes

Cast off 6 sts at beg of next 2 rows. 66(70:74:78:82:86) sts.
Next row: K2, skpo, k to last 4 sts, k2tog, K2.
Next row: P to end.
Rep the last 2 rows 2(2:3:3:4:4) times more. 60(64:66:70:72:76) sts.
Cont straight until back measures 52(53:54:55:56:57)cm (20½[21:21¼:21¾:22:22½]in) from cast on edge, ending with a p row.

Shape shoulders

Cast off 9(10:10:11:11:12) sts at beg of next 2 rows and 9(10:10:11:11:12) sts at beg of foll 2 rows.
Cast off rem 24(24:26:26:28:28) sts.

LEFT FRONT

With 5mm (US 8) needles and M cast on 42(44:46:48:50:52) sts.
Beg with a k row cont in St st until front measures 35(35:36:36:37:37)cm (13¾[13¾:14¼:14¼:14½:14½]in) from cast on edge, ending with a wrong side row.

Shape armhole

Cast off 6 sts at beg of next row. 36(38:40:42:44:46) sts.
Next row: P to end.
Next row: K2, skpo, k to end.
Rep the last 2 rows 2(2:3:3:4:4) times more. 33(35:36:38:39:41) sts.
Work straight until front measures 45(46:47:47:48:49)cm (17¾[18:18½:18½:19:19¼]in) from cast on edge, ending with a right side row.

Shape neck

Next row: Cast off 8 sts, p to end.
Dec one st at neck edge on every row until 18(20:20:22:22:24) sts rem.
Work straight until front measures same as back to shoulder, ending at side edge.

Shape shoulder

Cast off 9(10:10:11:11:12) sts at beg of next row.
Work 1 row.
Cast off rem 9(10:10:11:11:12) sts.

RIGHT FRONT

Mark positions for buttons on left front, the first 2cm (¾in) from cast on edge, the 7th 1cm (⅜in) from neck edge, the remaining 5 spaced evenly between. Work buttonholes on right front to correspond with markers as folls:

Buttonhole row (RS) K2, k2 tog, yf, k to end.

With 5mm (US 8) needles and M cast on 42(44:46:48:50:52) sts.

Beg with a k row cont in St st until front measures 35(35:36:36:37:37)cm (13¾[13¾:14¼:14¼:14½:14½]in) from cast on edge, ending with a wrong side row.

Shape armhole

Cast off 6 sts at beg of next row. 36(38:40:42:44:46) sts.

Next row: P to end.

Next row: K to last 4 sts, k2 tog, k2. Rep the last 2 rows 2(2:3:3:4:4) times more. 33(35:36:38:39:41) sts.

Work straight until front measures 45(46:47:47:48:49)cm (17¾[18:18½:18½:19:19¼]in) from cast on edge, ending with a right side row.

Shape neck

Next row: Cast off 8 sts, p to end.

Dec one st at neck edge on every row until 18(20:20:22:22:24) sts rem.

Work straight until front measures same as Back to shoulder, ending at side edge.

Shape shoulder

Cast off 9(10:10:11:11:12) sts at beg of next row.

Work 1 row.

Cast off rem 9(10:10:11:11:12) sts.

SLEEVES

With 5mm (US 8) needles and M cast on 36(38:40:42:44:46) sts.

Beg with a k row cont in St st.

Work 2 rows.

Inc row: K3, m1, k to last 3 sts, m1, k3.

Work 5 rows.

Rep the last 6 rows 7 times more, then inc on every foll 8th row until there are

62(64:66:68:70:72) sts.

Cont straight until sleeve measures 43(43:44:44:45:45)cm (17[17:17¼:17¼:17¾:17¾]in) from cast on edge, ending with a p row.

Shape top

Cast off 6 sts at beg of next 2 rows.

Next row: K2, skpo, k to last 4 sts, k2tog, K2.

Next row: P to end.

Rep these 2 rows 2(2:3:3:4:4) times more. Cast off.

COLLAR

Using 5mm (US 8) needles and M, cast on 107 sts.

K 1 row.

Dec row: 1(RS) K11, sl 1, k2 tog, psso, k to last 14 sts, sl 1, k2 tog, psso, k11.

K 1 row.

Dec row: 2 K10, sl 1, k2 tog, psso, k to last 13 sts, sl 1, k2 tog, psso, k10.

K 1 row.

Dec row: 3 K9, sl 1, k2 tog, psso, k to last 12 sts, sl 1, k2 tog, psso, k9.

K 1 row.

Cont in this way until 10 dec rows have been worked. 67 sts.

K 1 row.

Cast off 5 sts at beg of next 8 rows.

Cast off loosely.

LOWER BACK FACING

With 4½mm (US 7) needles, right side facing and C, pick up and k78(82:86:90:94:98) sts along cast on edge.

Next row: K to end.

Beg with a k row, work 8 rows St st.

Cast off.

SLEEVE FACINGS

With 4½mm (US 7) needles, right side facing and C, pick up and k36(38:40:42:44:46) sts along cast on edge.

Next row: K to end.

Beg with a k row, work 8 rows St st.

Cast off.

LOWER LEFT FRONT FACING

With 4½mm (US 7) needles, right side facing and C, pick up and k42(44:46:48:50:52) sts along cast on edge.

Next row: K to last st, inc in last st.
Next row: K1, skpo, k to end.
Next row: P to end.
Rep the last 2 rows 3 times more.
Cast off, decreasing on this row as before.

LEFT FRONT FACING

With 4½mm (US 7) needles, right side facing and C, pick up and k70(72:74:74:76:76) sts along front edge.

Next row: Inc in first st, k to end.
Next row: K to last 3 sts, k2tog, k1.
Next row: P to end.
Rep the last 2 rows 3 times more.
Cast off, decreasing this row as before.

LOWER RIGHT FRONT FACING

With 4½mm (US 7) needles, right side facing and C, pick up and k42(44:46:48:50:52) sts along cast on edge.

Next row: Inc in first st, k to end.
Next row: K to last 3 sts, k2tog, k1.
Next row: P to end.
Rep the last 2 rows 3 times more.
Cast off, decreasing on this row as before.

RIGHT FRONT FACING

Place markers opposite centre of buttonholes.

With 4½mm (US 7) needles, right side facing and C, pick up and k70(72:74:74:76:76) sts along front edge.

Next row: K to last st, inc in last st.
Next row: K1, skpo, k to end.
Next row: P to end.
Buttonhole row: K1, skpo, k2tog, y2rn, skpo, [k to within 2 sts of marker, skpo, k2tog, y2rn, skpo] 6 times, k to end.
Next row: P to end.
Next row: K1, skpo, k to end.

Next row: P to end.
Rep the last 2 rows once more.
Cast off, decreasing on this row as before.

TO FINISH

Join shoulder seams. With centre of sleeves to shoulder seam, sew on sleeves. Join side and sleeve seams. Join facing seams at lower edge of fronts. Fold all facings to wrong side and sew in place. Sew on buttons.

LINING

To cut lining, fold all facings to wrong side and use knitted pieces as a template.

Fold back in half down centre back. With lining folded in half, place centre of back on lining 2.5cm (1in) from folded edge of lining.

Place one front on lining with centre front parallel to selvedge.

Place one sleeve on double lining. Allowing a 2cm (¾in) seam along all edges, cut out lining.

Make pleat in centre back by sewing 8cm (3in) down from neck and up from lower edge and 2.5cm (1in) from fold.

Join side and shoulder seams.

Join sleeve seams.

Sew sleeves into armhole. Make a second seam 6mm (¼in) from first seam. Snip to seam all round armhole at 12mm (½in) spaces.

Machine stitch around the neck edge, then snip to seam all the way around the neck edge.

With wrong sides together, place lining inside Jacket. Fold 2cm (¾in) to wrong side all round lining and slip stitch in place, just below casted off edge of facings and along seam edge at neck.

Twirl-Top Evening Bag

MATERIALS

5 balls of Handknit Cotton by Rowan in (A), 85m/50g, 100% cotton
1 ball Kidsilk Haze by Rowan in Heavenly (B), 210m/25g, 70% super kid mohair/30% silk
5.5mm (US 9) needles and a 5.5mm (US 9) circular needle.

TENSION

14 sts and 18 rows to 10cm (4in) square over St st on 5.5mm (US 9) needles.

MEASUREMENTS

Width: 25cm (10in)
Height: 25cm (10in)
Depth: 10cm (4in)

FRONT AND BACK

Using 2 strands of A and 1 strand of B and 5.5mm (US 9) needles, cast on 35 sts.
Work 4 rows in garter stitch.
Change to St st and work until piece measures 25cm (10in).
Leave sts on a spare needle.

SIDE PANEL

Using 2 strands of A and 1 strand of B and 5.5mm (US 9) needles, cast on 14 sts.
Work in garter stitch until work measures 25cm (10in).
Change to St st and work 12 rows straight.
Dec 1st at each end of next and every following 4th row until 6 sts remain, then cont until work measures 50cm (20in).
Leave sts on a spare needle or a thread.
Return to the cast on edge of the side panel and pick up and knit 14 sts along cast on edge.
Work as given for other side of panel.

TOP EDGE

Using 5.5mm (US 9) circular needle, knit 6 sts of side panel, 35 sts of front panel, 6 sts of other side panel and finally 35 sts of back panel.
Working in a circle, work 3 rows in k2, p2 rib.
Next row: Working in rib as set, make eyelet holes on every alt knit st by k2tog, yfwd all the way around the bag.
Work another 3 rows in rib.
Change to St st and work to rows.
Next row: Inc 1st in every st across all sts.
Work 4 rows in St st and repeat inc row once more.
Work 2 rows in St st.
Change to 2 strands of B only and cast off.
Join all seams and stitch the frilled edge into pleats as shown in the picture.
Make an I-cord, as shown on page 83, using yarns as used throughout the bag until the cord is long enough to thread through the bag and tie.

Cardigan

MATERIALS

10(11:11:12:12:13) balls of Wool Cotton by Rowan, 113m/50gm, 50% wool/50% cotton
Pair of 3¼mm (US 4) and 4mm (US 6) knitting needles.
7 Buttons

MEASUREMENTS

To fit bust:

| 81 | 86 | 92 | 97 | 102 | 107 | cm |
| 32 | 34 | 36 | 38 | 40 | 42 | in |

Actual measurements

Bust

| 92 | 98 | 103 | 108 | 114 | 120 | cm |
| 36¼ | 38½ | 40½ | 42½ | 45 | 47¼ | in |

Length to shoulder

| 63 | 64 | 65 | 66 | 67 | 68 | cm |
| 25 | 25¼ | 25¾ | 26 | 26½ | 27 | in |

Sleeve length

| 43 | 43 | 44 | 44 | 45 | 45 | cm |
| 17 | 17 | 17¼ | 17¼ | 17¾ | 17¾ | in |

TENSION

22 sts and 30 rows to 10cm (4in) square over St st on 4mm (US 6) needles.

ABBREVIATIONS

See page 109.

BACK

With 4mm (US 6) needles, cast on 104(110:116:122:128:134) sts.
Moss st row 1: * K1, p1; rep from * to end.
Moss st row 2: * P1, k1, rep from * to end.
Rep the last 2 rows 4 times more.
Change to 4mm (US 6) needles.
Beg with a k row cont in St st until back measures 63(64:65:66:67:68)cm (25[25¼:25¾:26:26½:27]in) from cast on edge, ending with a p row.
Shape shoulder
Next 4 rows: Work to last 12(13:14:15:16:17) sts, turn.

Next 2 rows: Work to last 10(10:11:11:12:12) sts, turn.
Cast off centre 36(38:38:40:40:42) sts.

POCKETS (make 2)

With 4mm (US 6) needles, cast on 30(32:32:34:34:36) sts.
Beg with a k row, work 38(38:40:40:42:42) rows in St st.
Change to 3¼mm (US 4) needles.
Moss st row 1: * K1, p1; rep from * to end.
Moss st row 2: * P1, k1, rep from * to end.
Rep the last 2 rows once more.
Cast off in moss st.

LEFT FRONT

With 3¼mm (US 4) needles, cast on 48(52:54:58:60:64) sts.
Moss st row 1: * K1, p1; rep from * to end.
Moss st row 2: * P1, k1, rep from * to end.
Rep the last 2 rows 4 times more.
Change to 4mm (US 6) needles.
Beg with a k row cont in St st until front measures 55(56:56:57:57:58)cm (22¾[22:22:22½:22½:22¾]in) from cast on edge, ending with a p row.
Shape neck
Next row: K to last 10(10:11:11:12:12) sts, turn and leave these sts on a holder for collar.
Dec one st at neck edge on every foll alt row until 34(36:39:41:44:46) sts rem.
Work straight until front matches back to shoulder shaping, ending at side edge.
Shape shoulder
Next row: K to end.
Next row: P to last 12(13:14:15:16:17) sts, turn.
Rep the last 2 rows once more.
Next row: P to end.
Leave these sts on a spare needle.

RIGHT FRONT

With 3¼mm (US 3) needles, cast on 48(52:54:58:60:64) sts.

Moss st row 1: * K1, p1; rep from * to end.

Moss st row 2: * P1, k1, rep from * to end.

Rep the last 2 rows 4 times more.
Change to 4mm (US 6) needles.
Beg with a k row cont in St st until front measures 55(56:56:57:57:58)cm (22¾[22:22:22½:22½:22¾]in) from cast on edge, ending with a p row.

Shape neck

Next row: K10(10:11:11:12:12) sts, leave these sts on a holder for collar, k to end.
Dec one st at neck edge on every foll alt row until 34(36:39:41:44:46) sts rem.
Work straight until front matches back to shoulder shaping, ending at side edge.

Shape shoulder

Next row: P to end.
Next row: K to last 11(12:13:14:15:16) sts, turn.
Rep the last 2 rows once more.
Next row: P to end.
Leave these sts on a spare needle.

SLEEVES

With 3¼mm (US 3) needles, cast on 42(46:50:54:58:62) sts.
Work 8 rows moss st as given for back.
Change to 4mm (US 6) needles.
Beg with a k row, cont in St st.
Work 2 rows.
Inc row: K3, m1, k to last 3 sts, m1, k3.
Work 5 rows.
Rep the last 6 rows until there are 80(84:88:92:96:100) sts.
Cont straight until Sleeve measures 43(43:44:44:45:45)cm (17[17:17¼:17¼:17¾:17¾]in) from cast on edge, ending with a p row.
Cast off.

BUTTON BAND

With US 3 (3¼mm) needles and right side facing, pick up and

k128(130:130:132:132:134) sts evenly along left front edge.

Moss st row 1: * K1, p1; rep from * to end.

Moss st row 2: * P1, k1, rep from * to end.

Rep the last 2 rows 3 times more.
Cast off in moss st.

BUTTONHOLE BAND

With 3¼mm (US 3) needles and right side facing, pick up and k128(130:130:132:132:134) sts evenly along left front edge.

Moss st row 1: * K1, p1; rep from * to end.

Moss st row 2: * P1, k1, rep from * to end.

Work 1 more row.

1st buttonhole row: Moss st 5(7:7:9:9:11), [work 2 tog, y2rn, work 2 tog, moss st 15] 6 times, work 2 tog, y2rn, work 2 tog, moss st 5.

2nd buttonhole row: Moss st to end, working twice in y2rn.
Moss st 3 more rows.
Cast off in moss st.

COLLAR

With 3¼mm (US 3) needles cast on 140(144:144:148:148:152) sts.
Work 7cm (3in) in moss st as given for back.
Cast off 12 sts at beg of next 8 rows.
Cast off rem 32 sts.

TO FINISH

Join right shoulder seams as follows:
With point of needles facing neck edges, place sts from left back shoulder and left front shoulder each onto a 4mm (US 6) needle. With the right side of back and front together, and using a third 4mm (US 6) needle, knit the first st from each needle together, then knit the second st from each needle together, pass the first stitch over the second stitch and off the needle, knit the third st from each needle together,

pass the second stitch over the third stitch and off the needle, cont in this way until all the stitches have been cast off.

Starting and ending at inside edge of front bands, sew cast off edge of collar in place. Sew on sleeves. Join side and sleeve seams. Sew on buttons. Sew pockets to fronts.

ALTERNATIVE FRONTS (with knitted up borders and integral pockets)

POCKET LININGS

With 3¼mm (US 3) needles, cast on 30(32:32:34:34:36) sts.
Beg with a k row, work 38(38:40:40:42:42) rows in St st.
Leave these sts on a holder.

LEFT FRONT

With 3¼mm (US 3) needles, cast on 58(62:64:68:70:74) sts.
Moss st row 1: * K1, p1; rep from * to end.
Moss st row 2: * P1, k1, rep from * to end.
Rep the last 2 rows 4 times more.
Change to 4mm (US 6) needles.
Next row: K to last 11 sts, inc in next st, turn and leave these sts on a holder for button band. 49(53:55:59:61:65) sts.
Beg with a p row, work 37(37:39:39:41:41) rows in St st.
Pocket opening
Next row: K10(12:13:15:15: 17), slip next 30 (32: 32: 34: 34: 36) sts on a holder, k across 30(32:32:34:34:36) sts of pocket lining, k9(9:10:10:12:12).
Beg with a p row cont in St st until front measures 55(56:56:57:57:58)cm (22¾[22:22:22½:22½:22¾]in) from cast on edge, ending with a k row.
Shape neck
Next row: Cast off 10(10:11:11:12:12) sts, p to end.
Dec one st at neck edge on every foll alt

row until 34(36:39:41:44:46) sts rem.
Work straight until front matches back to shoulder shaping, ending at side edge.
Shape shoulder
Next row: K to end.
Next row: P to last 11(12:13:14:15:16) sts, turn.
Rep the last 2 rows once more.
Next row: K to end.
Leave these sts on a spare needle.

RIGHT FRONT

With 3¼mm (US 3) needles cast on 58(62:64:68:70:74) sts.
Moss st row 1: * K1, p1; rep from * to end.
Moss st row 2: * P1, k1, rep from * to end.
Rep the last 2 rows once more.
1st buttonhole row: Moss st 3, work 2 tog, y2rn, work 2 tog, moss st to end.
2nd buttonhole row: Moss st to end, working twice in y2rn.
Work 2 more rows moss st.
Change to 4mm (US 6) needles.
Next row: Moss st 10, leave these sts on a holder for buttonhole band, inc in next st. 49(53:55:59:61:65) sts.
Beg with a p row, work 37(37:39:39:41:41) rows in St st.
Pocket opening
Next row: K9(9:10:10:12:12), slip next 30 (32:32:34:34:36) sts on a holder, k across 30(32:32:34:34:36) sts of pocket lining, k10(12:13:15:15:17).
Beg with a p row cont in St st until front measures 55(56:56:57 57:58)cm (22¾[22:22:22½:22½:22¾]in) from cast on edge, ending with a k row.
Shape neck
Next row: Cast off 10(10:11:11:12:12) sts, p to end.
Dec one st at neck edge on every foll alt row until 34(36:39:41:44:46) sts rem.
Work straight until front matches back to shoulder shaping, ending at side edge.

Shape shoulder
Next row: K to end.
Next row: P to last 11(12:13:14:15:16) sts, turn.
Rep the last 2 rows once more.
Next row: K to end.
Leave these sts on a spare needle.

BUTTON BAND

With right side facing, using 3¼mm (US 3) needles, rejoin yarn to sts left on a holder for button band.
Next row: Inc in first st, moss st to end. 11 sts.
Cont in moss st until band, when slightly stretched, fits up left front to beg of neck shaping, ending with a right side row.
Cast off in moss st.
Sew in place.

BUTTONHOLE BAND

Place markers for buttons on buttonhole band, the first level with buttonhole worked on right front, the seventh 2cm (¾in) from top edge, the rem 5 spaced evenly between.
With wrong side facing, using 3¼mm (US 3) needles, rejoin yarn to sts left on a holder for button band.
Next row: Inc in first st, moss st to end. 11 sts.
Cont in moss st, working buttonholes to match buttonholes already worked, until band when slightly stretched, fits up left front to beg of neck shaping, ending with a right side row.
Cast off in moss st.
Sew in place.

POCKET TOPS

With right side facing, using 3¼mm (US 3) needles, place sts of pocket front on a needle, work 4 rows moss st as given for back.
Cast off in moss st.
Sew in place.

Zip-Front Cardigan

MATERIALS

5(6:6:7:7:8) balls of All Seasons
Cotton by Rowan in Pansy (M).
90m/50g, 60% cotton/40%
acrylic/microfibre
2 balls in Soul (C)
Pair of 4mm (US 6) and 5mm
(US 8) knitting needles.
50(50:50:55:55:55)cm
(20[20:20:22:22:22]in) open-ended
zip.

MEASUREMENTS

To fit bust:

81	86	92	97	102	107	cm
32	34	36	38	40	42	in

Actual measurements

Bust

92	98	103	108	114	120	cm
36¼	38½	40½	42½	45	47¼	in

Length to shoulder

47	47	47	52	52	52	cm
18½	18½	18½	20½	20½	20½	in

Sleeve length

43	43	44	44	45	45	cm
17	17	17¼	17¼	17¾	17¾	in

TENSION

17 sts and 24 rows to 10cm (4in)
square over St st using 5mm (US 8)
needles.

ABBREVIATIONS

See page 109.

BACK

With 4mm (US 6) needles and M, cast
on 82(86:90:94:98:102) sts.
1st, 3rd and 5th sizes only
1st rib row: K2, * p2, k2; rep from *
to end.
2nd rib row: P2, * k2, p2; rep from *
to end.
2nd, 4th and 6th sizes only
1st rib row: P2, * k2, p2; rep from *
to end.
2nd rib row: K2, * p2, k2; rep from *

to end.
These 2 rows form the rib.
All sizes
Cont in stripes of 4 rows M, 2 rows C
and 4 rows M, 2 rows C, and 6 rows M.
Change to 5mm (US 8) needles.
Beg with a k row cont in St st and M
only until back measures
30(29:28:32:31:30)cm
(11¾[11½:11:12½:12¼:11¾]in) from cast
on edge, ending with a wrong side row.
Shape armholes
Cast off 6 sts at beg of next 2 rows.
70(74:78:82:86:90) sts.
Next row: K2, skpo, k to last 4 sts,
k2tog, K2.
Next row: P to end.
Rep the last 2 rows 2(2:3:3:4:4) times
more. 64(68:70:74:76:80) sts.
Cont straight until back measures
44(44:44:49:49:49)cm
(17¼[17¼:17¼:19¼:19¼:19¼]in) from
cast on edge, ending with a p row.
Shape back neck
Next row: K23(24:25:26:27:28) sts, turn
and work on these sts for first side of
front neck.
Dec one st at neck edge of the next 4
rows. Work 3 rows straight.
Shape shoulder
Cast off 10(10:11:11:12:12) sts at beg of
next row.
Work 1 row.
Cast off rem 9(10:10:11:11:12) sts.
With right side facing, slip centre
18(20:20:22:22:24) sts on a holder, join
on yarn, k to end.
Dec one st at neck edge of the next
4 rows.
Work 4 rows straight.
Shape shoulder
Cast off 10(10:11:11:12:12) sts at beg of
next row.
Work 1 row.
Cast off rem 9(10:10:11:11:12) sts.

LEFT FRONT

With 4mm (US 6) needles and M, cast
on 39(41:43:45:47:49) sts.

Shape neck

Next row: K to last 8 sts, turn and leave these sts on a holder.

Dec one st at neck edge on every row until 19(20:21:22:23:24) sts rem.

Work straight until front measures same as back to shoulder, ending at side edge.

Shape shoulder

Cast off 10(10:11:11:12:12) sts at beg of next row.

Work 1 row.

Cast off rem 9(10:10:11:11:12) sts.

RIGHT FRONT

With 4mm (US 6) needles and M, cast on 39(41:43:45:47:49) sts.

1st and 3rd sizes only

1st rib row: K3, * p2, k2; rep from * to end.

2nd rib row: P2, * k2, p2; rep from * to last 5 sts, k5.

2nd size only

1st rib row: K3, * p2, k2, rep from * to last 2 sts, p2.

2nd rib row: K2, * p2, k2; rep from * to last 7 sts, p2, k5.

These 2 rows form the rib with g st edging.

All sizes

Cont in stripes of 4 rows M, 2 rows C and 4 rows M, 2 rows C, and 6 rows M.

Change to 5mm (US 8) needles.

Cont in M only.

Next row: K to end.

Next row: P to last 3 sts, k3.

These 2 rows form the St st with g st border.

Rep the last 2 rows front measures 30(29:28:32:31:30)cm (11¾[11½:11:12½:12¼:11¾]in) from cast on edge, ending with a right side row.

Shape armhole

Cast off 6 sts at beg of next row. 33(35:37:39:41:43) sts.

Next row: K to last 4 sts, k2 tog, k2.

Next row: P to last 3 sts, k3.

Rep the last 2 rows 2(2:3:3:4:4) times more. 36(38:39:41:42:44) sts.

1st, 3rd and 5th sizes only

1st rib row: K2, * p2, k2; rep from * to last 5 sts, p2, k3.

2nd rib row: K5, p2, * k2, p2; rep from * to end.

2nd, 4th and 6th sizes only

1st rib row: P2, * k2, p2, rep from * to last 3 sts, k3.

2nd rib row: K5, *p2, k2; rep from * to end.

These 2 rows form the rib with g st edging.

All sizes

Cont in stripes of 4 rows M, 2 rows C and 4 rows M, 2 rows C, and 6 rows M.

Change to 5mm (US 8) needles.

Cont in M only.

Next row: K to end.

Next row: K3, p to end.

These 2 rows form the St st with g st border.

Rep the last 2 rows front measures 30(29:28:32:31:30)cm (11¾[11½:11:12½:12¼:11¾]in) from cast on edge, ending with a wrong side row.

Shape armhole

Cast off 6 sts at beg of next row. 33(35:37:39:41:43) sts.

Next row: K3, p to end.

Next row: K2, skpo, k to end.

Next row: K3, p to end.

Rep the last 2 rows 2(2:3:3:4:4) times more. 36(38:39:41:42:44) sts.

Work straight until front measures 42(42:42:47:47:47)cm (16½[16½:16½:18½:18½:18½]in) from cast on edge, ending with a p row.

Work straight until front measures 42(42:42:47:47:47)cm (16½[16½:16½:18½:18½:18½]in) from cast on edge, ending with a p row.

Shape neck

Next row: K8 sts, leave these sts on a holder, then k to end.

Dec one st at neck edge on every row until 19(20:21:22:23:24) sts rem.

Work straight until front measures same as Back to shoulder, ending at side edge.

Shape shoulder

Cast off 10(10:11:11:12:12) sts at beg of next row.

Work 1 row.

Cast off rem 9(10:10:11:11:12) sts.

SLEEVES

With 4mm (US 6) needles and M, cast on 38(42:42:46:46:50) sts.

1st rib row: K2, * p2, k2; rep from * to end.

2nd rib row: P2, * k2, p2; rep from * to end.

These 2 rows form the rib.

All sizes

Cont in stripes of 4 rows M, 2 rows C and 4 rows M, 2 rows C, and 6 rows M.

Change to 5mm (US 8) needles.

Cont in M only.

Beg with a k row cont in St st.

Work 2 rows.

Inc row: K3, m1, k to last 3 sts, m1, k3.

Work 5 rows.

Rep the last 6 rows until there are 64(68:72:74:78:82) sts.

Cont straight until sleeve measures 43(43:44:44:45:45)cm (17[17:17¼:17¼:17¾:17¾]in) from cast on edge, ending with a p row.

Shape top

Cast off 6 sts at beg of next 2 rows.

Next row: K2, skpo, k to last 4 sts, k2tog, K2.

Next row: P to end.

Rep the last 2 rows 2(2:3:3:4:4) times more.

Cast off.

COLLAR

Join shoulder seams.

With 4½mm (US 7) needles and M, slip 8 sts from holder onto needle, pick up and k12(13:13:14:16:17) sts up right front neck, 11 sts from right back neck, k18(20:20:22:22:24) sts from back neck holder, pick up and k11 sts from left back neck, 12(13:13:14:16:17) sts down left front neck, k8 from holder. 80(84:84:88:92:96) sts.

Next row: K3, * p2, k2; rep from * to last 5 sts, p2, k3.

Next row: K5, p2, * k2, p2; rep from * to last 5 sts, k5.

These 2 rows set the rib patt.

Work a further 3 rows M, 2 rows C, 4 rows M, 2 rows C, 5 rows M.

Next row: K3, * p2 tog, k2; rep from * to last 5 sts, p2 tog, k3. 61(64:64:67:70:73) sts.

Next row: Cast off 1 st, k to end.

Next row: Cast off 1 st, p to last st, k1. 59(62:62:65:68:71) sts.

Next row: K to end.

Next row: K1, p to last st, k1.

Rep the last 2 rows 7 times more.

Next row: K4, leave these sts on a safety pin, cast off loosely the next 51(54:54:57:60:63) sts, k to end.

Cont on these 4 sts for zip facing.

Next row: K1, p2, k1.

Next row: K to end.

Rep the last 2 rows until facing is 42(42:42:47:47:47)cm (16½[16½:16½:18½:18½:18½]in) long.

Cast off.

With wrong side facing, rejoin yarn to rem sts.

Work to match first zip facing.

TO FINISH

With centre of sleeves to shoulder seam, sew on sleeves. Join side and sleeve seams. Sew in zip to halfway up collar. Fold collar in half and slip stitch in place. Sew zip facings in place over zip tape.

Technical

I've included a needle conversion list and abbreviations and the terms used throughout the book. All projects were knit in Rowan Yarns. If you would like additional information, visit the Rowan website or contract the distributor.

Knitting Needle Conversion table

UK (mm)	1¾	2	2¼	2¾	3	3¼	3½	3¾	4	4½	5	5½	6	6½	7	7½	8	9	10
US (size)		0	1	2		3	4	5	6	7	8	9	10	10½			11	13	15
CAN (size)	15	14	13	12	11	10		9	8	7	6	5	4	3	2	1	0	00	000

circular needle chart

1 inch	10cm	40cm	50cm	60cm	70cm	80cm	100cm	120cm
3	12	56	69	81	95	109	136	160
4	16	72	89	105	123	141	176	208
4½	18	80	99	117	137	157	196	232
5	20	88	109	129	151	173	216	256
5½	22	96	119	141	165	189	236	280
6	24	104	129	153	179	205	255	303
6½	26	112	138	164	192	220	275	327
7	28	120	148	176	206	236	294	350
7½	30	128	158	188	220	252	314	374
8	32	136	168	200	234	268	334	398
8½	34	144	178	212	248	284	353	421
9	36	152	188	224	262	300	373	445

Abbreviations

alt	alternate
beg	beginning/begin
cont	continue
cm	centimetre
c4b	cable 4 back: slip next 2 sts onto a cable needle and hold at back of work, k2, then k2 from the cable needle
c4f	cable 4 front: slip next 2 sts onto a cable needle and hold at front of work, k2, then k2 from the cable needle
c6b	cable 6 back: slip next 3 sts onto a cable needle and hold at back of work, k3, then k3 from the cable needle
dec	decrease
g	grams
in	inch
inc	increase
k	knit
k2tog	knit two stitches together
mb	make bobble: using yarn B, (k1, p1) twice into next st, (turn, p4, turn, k4) twice, turn, p4, turn and sl2, k2tog, psso
mm	millimetre
m1	make one stitch
oz	ounces

p	purl
patt	pattern
pb	place bead: yarn forward, slip bead to front of work, slip 1 st purlwise, take yarn to back of work. Bead will now be sitting in front of slipped stitch
ps	Place sequin: yarn forward, slip sequin to front of work, slip 1 st purlwise, take yarn to back of work. Sequin will now be sitting in front of the slipped stitch
psso	pass slipped stitch over
p2tog	purl two stitches together
rem	remaining
rep	repeat
RS	right side of work
skpo	slip 1, knit 1, pass slip stitch over
sl	slip
St st	stocking (stockinette) stitch
st/sts	stitch/stitches
WS	wrong side of work
y2rn	yarn round needle twice
yb	yarn back
yf	yarn forward
k	repeat instructions between k as many times as instructed
*	repeat instructions between * as many times as instructed

Rowan Yarns

UK
Rowan Yarns and Jaeger Handknits
Green Lane Mill
Holmfirth, West Yorkshire
HD9 2DX
Tel: 01484 681881
www.knitrowan.com

USA
Westminster Fibers, Inc.
165 Ledge St.
Nashua, NH 03063
1-800-445-9276
www.westminsterfibers.com
rowan@westminsterfibers.com

CANADA
Diamond Yarn (Montreal)
9697 St Laurent
Montreal, Quebec H3L 2N1
Tel: (514) 388 6188

Diamond Yarn (Toronto)
155 Martin Ross, Unit 3
Toronto, Ontario M3J 2L9
Tel: (416) 736 6111

AUSTRALIA
Rowan at Sunspun
185 Canterbury Road
Canterbury
Victoria 3126
Tel: 03 9830 1609

Index

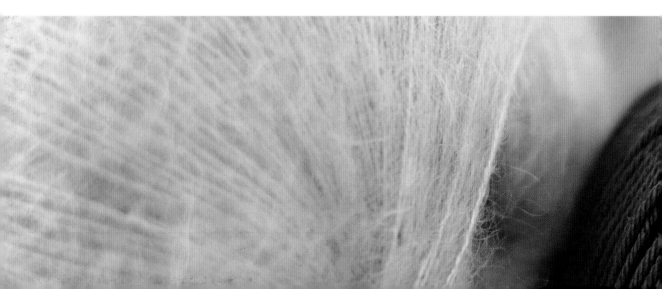

Acknowledgements

I would like to thank all the people that have supported me while writing this book:

Kate Buller for taking me on as a Design Consultant ten years ago and making these opportunities possible to me.

Katie Cowan at Collins & Brown for making this project a reality and Rowan Yarns for the support with yarn.

I'd like to extend my gratitude to **Penny Hill** for helping with the making of the garments and technical support during the photography.

Michael Wicks for his patience and the great photography he produced.

I'd also like to thank **Michelle Lo** for her support throughout the process.

Moreover, to **my mother** who is always there when I need her and to **my dad** who is always there with a glass of wine after a tough day.

Last, but not least, to **my niece Natasha** for making my nails look fab for the photography.

All photography by Michael Wicks.

Love crafts? Crafters… keep updated on all exciting craft news from Collins & Brown. Email **lovecrafts@anovabooks.com** to register for **free** email alerts on forthcoming titles and author events.